AF787727

Critical Infrastructure - Modern Approach and New Developments

Edited by Antonio Di Pietro and Josè Martì

Published in London, United Kingdom

Critical Infrastructure - Modern Approach and New Developments
http://dx.doi.org/10.5772/intechopen.104070
Edited by Antonio Di Pietro and Josè Martì

Contributors
Clemente Fuggini, Miltiadis Kontogeorgos, Fabio Bolletta, Saimir Osmani, Sandra Gesing, Marlon Pierce, Suresh Marru, Michael Zentner, Kathryn Huff, Shannon Bradley, Sean B. Cleveland, Steven R. Brandt, Rajiv Ramnath, Kerk Kee, Maytal Dahan, Braulio M. Villegas Martinez, Jose J. Sánchez Mondragón, Christina Nikolova, Ashtarout Ammar, Hala Nassereddine, Gabriel Dadi, Antonio Di Pietro, José Martí, Alessandro Calabrese, Antonio De Nicola, Daniele Ferneti, Luisa Franchina, Tommaso Ruocco

© The Editor(s) and the Author(s) 2024

The rights of the editor(s) and the author(s) have been asserted in accordance with the Copyright, Designs and Patents Act 1988. All rights to the book as a whole are reserved by INTECHOPEN LIMITED. The book as a whole (compilation) cannot be reproduced, distributed or used for commercial or non-commercial purposes without INTECHOPEN LIMITED's written permission. Enquiries concerning the use of the book should be directed to INTECHOPEN LIMITED rights and permissions department (permissions@intechopen.com).

Violations are liable to prosecution under the governing Copyright Law.

Individual chapters of this publication are distributed under the terms of the Creative Commons Attribution 3.0 Unported License which permits commercial use, distribution and reproduction of the individual chapters, provided the original author(s) and source publication are appropriately acknowledged. If so indicated, certain images may not be included under the Creative Commons license. In such cases users will need to obtain permission from the license holder to reproduce the material. More details and guidelines concerning content reuse and adaptation can be found at http://www.intechopen.com/copyright-policy.html.

Notice

Statements and opinions expressed in the chapters are these of the individual contributors and not necessarily those of the editors or publisher. No responsibility is accepted for the accuracy of information contained in the published chapters. The publisher assumes no responsibility for any damage or injury to persons or property arising out of the use of any materials, instructions, methods or ideas contained in the book.

First published in London, United Kingdom, 2024 by IntechOpen
IntechOpen is the global imprint of INTECHOPEN LIMITED, registered in England and Wales, registration number: 11086078, 5 Princes Gate Court, London, SW7 2QJ, United Kingdom

British Library Cataloguing-in-Publication Data
A catalogue record for this book is available from the British Library

Additional hard and PDF copies can be obtained from orders@intechopen.com

Critical Infrastructure - Modern Approach and New Developments
Edited by Antonio Di Pietro and Josè Martì
p. cm.
Print ISBN 978-1-83768-107-5
Online ISBN 978-1-83768-108-2
eBook (PDF) ISBN 978-1-83768-109-9

We are IntechOpen, the world's leading publisher of Open Access books

Built by scientists, for scientists

6,800+
Open access books available

183,000+
International authors and editors

200M+
Downloads

156
Countries delivered to

Our authors are among the
Top 1%
most cited scientists

12.2%
Contributors from top 500 universities

WEB OF SCIENCE™

Selection of our books indexed in the Book Citation Index
in Web of Science™ Core Collection (BKCI)

Interested in publishing with us?
Contact book.department@intechopen.com

Numbers displayed above are based on latest data collected.
For more information visit www.intechopen.com

For EU product safety concerns:
IN TECH d.o.o., Prolaz Marije Krucifikse Kozulić 3, 51000 Rijeka, Croatia,
info@intechopen.com or visit our website at intechopen.com.

Meet the editors

Antonio Di Pietro earned his master's degree in Informatics Engineering at Sapienza University of Rome in 2004 and his Ph.D. in the same field at Roma Tre University in 2015. He has been working as a researcher at the Italian National Agency for New Technologies, Energy and Sustainable Economic Development (ENEA) since 2007. His current research activities include the modelling and simulation of critical infrastructures and the development of decision support systems integrating natural hazard modelling. He took part in several European and Italian national research projects and acted as an advisor in some evaluation studies commissioned by the European Union in the field of critical infrastructure protection. Dr. Di Pietro has been the advisor of several MSc students and a professor in software engineering, programming language databases, cases, and distributed applications courses.

José R. Martí has a Ph.D. in Electrical Engineering from the University of British Columbia (UBC), Vancouver, Canada. He is a professor at this institution, where he has made contributions to real-time solutions of large power networks and the modelling of interdependent critical infrastructures for resiliency and real-time response. Contributions include models for travelling wave propagation of electromagnetic waves, hydraulic waves, seismic waves, and wildfire spread. He is the lead investigator of the Complex Systems Integration (CSI) Laboratory at the Institute for Computing, Information and Cognitive Systems (ICICS) at UBC. Current projects include considering the effect of climate change in risk evaluation, real-time earthquake early warning preparation and response, and real-time wildfire spread and suppression.

Contents

Preface **IX**

Section 1
Introduction **1**

Chapter 1 **3**
Introductory Chapter: Critical Infrastructure – Modern Approach
and New Developments
by Antonio Di Pietro and Josè Martì

Section 2
Analysis of Critical Infrastructures: Risk Identification and Reduction **9**

Chapter 2 **11**
Resilience of Infrastructures and Systems to Multiple Hazardous Events:
Application Cases and Future Perspectives
*by Clemente Fuggini, Miltiadis Kontogeorgos, Saimir Osmani
and Fabio Bolletta*

Chapter 3 **31**
An Open-Data-Based Methodology for the Creation of a Graph of Critical
Infrastructure Dependencies at an Urban Scale
*by Antonio Di Pietro, Alessandro Calabrese, Antonio De Nicola,
Daniele Ferneti, Luisa Franchina, Josè Martì and Tommaso Ruocco*

Chapter 4 **47**
Science Gateways and AI/ML: How Can Gateway Concepts and Solutions
Meet the Needs in Data Science?
*by Sandra Gesing, Marlon Pierce, Suresh Marru, Michael Zentner, Kathryn Huff,
Shannon Bradley, Sean B. Cleveland, Steven R. Brandt, Rajiv Ramnath, Kerk Kee,
Maytal Dahan, Braulio M. Villegas Martínez, Wilmer Contreras Sepulveda
and José J. Sánchez Mondragón*

Section 3
Sustainable and Digital Twin-Based Approaches for the Transport Infrastructure **69**

Chapter 5 **71**
Providing Sustainable Transport Infrastructure through Internalization of External Costs: A Case Study from South-Eastern European Countries
by Christina Nikolova

Chapter 6 **97**
Perspective Chapter: Roadmap to a Holistic Highway Digital Twin – A Why, How, and Why Framework
by Ashtarout Ammar, Hala Nassereddine and Gabriel Dadi

Preface

Global warming and natural and humanmade disasters are becoming more frequent and devastating to life and infrastructures. There are two types of natural disasters: uncontrollable and controllable. Uncontrollable disasters include earthquakes, tsunamis, windstorms, hurricanes, and others, for which the event's evolution is determined by nature, and when the disaster strikes, our responses are limited to early warning and repair actions. Controllable disasters are those like wildfires, floods, and pandemics, for which, in addition to early warning and repair actions, we can also modify the evolution of the event (e.g., wildfires, pandemics). Humanmade disasters (e.g., cybersecurity) and disasters caused by building code deficiencies and violations are, to some degree, avoidable. By their nature, cities are the most vulnerable assets and suffer the most consequences during disasters. More and smarter investments should be applied to city designs (smart cities) to make them more robust.

Examples of critical systems include electrical and telecommunication systems. These systems allow mobile transportation, stoplights, light detectors, and railways that compose the modern transportation sector. If the electricity supply is not available, then the operations of these other systems will also be impacted. Failures in the telecommunication system, for example, due to cyberattacks or physical internal failures, can paralyze the services of an entire city. Although there are several definitions of resilience, we could define resilience as the capacity of a system to prepare for critical events, maintain the system's functionality as much as possible when the event happens, and recover the functionality as soon as possible. In engineering literature, resilience plays a decisive role in the study of critical infrastructures (CIs). However, most research regarding the resilience of critical infrastructure systems focuses on single, isolated systems, such as the electric grid, transportation, or water, without consideration of surrounding systems. Since CIs are interdependent, these models fail to assess the resilience of the system of systems.

To strengthen resilience, it is necessary to improve the risk culture and integrate resilience into the strategic design process. Risk management includes five pillars: preparedness, mitigation, response, recovery, and evaluation. Preparedness refers to building following building codes and alternative supply links and backup strategies, training personnel for rapid response after the event, and providing educational activities for the public regarding what to do during potentially disastrous events. Mitigation refers to actions to prevent or reduce the disasters' cause, impact, and consequences. The response phase occurs in the immediate aftermath of a disaster. When a disaster occurs, actions are taken to save lives, treat injuries, and minimize the effects of the disaster. During the recovery period, restoration efforts occur concurrently with regular operations and activities. Finally, evaluation includes actions to review the response effectiveness and reactions in preparation for the next disaster.

Regardless of the type of disaster, the timeline of a disaster can be divided into three periods: pre-disaster (preparedness and mitigation), during the disaster (response and recovery), and post-disaster (evaluation).

The post-disaster period can be more finely divided into hours after, days after, weeks after, and months after the disaster strikes. The faster the response, the less the total consequences of the disaster will be in terms of monetary losses and social and personal impacts. Even though much effort should be put into the response in the hours immediately after the disaster (when most lives are at stake), the preparation and post-disaster periods can strongly influence the total losses suffered in the disaster. Reinforcement of the system before the disaster increases the robustness of citizens and infrastructures. Reinforcement includes preparing citizens how to protect their lives during the event, reinforcing buildings and homes, and reinforcing CIs. The decisions made regarding which assets to prioritize for a given CI budget will depend on the role of that asset in preventing loss of life and restoring the quality of life after the disaster.

A targeted and prioritized response immediately after the disaster requires knowing where the victims are located, the severity of their injuries, the transportation time, and the availability of treatment in the hospitals. The subsequent short-term and mid-term periods after the disaster focus on recovering infrastructure to restore people's well-being to a minimum level. The actions during the first days after the disaster will considerably impact the total time until a minimum functionality of the system is achieved. This period can be shortened from several weeks to a few days by increasing the efficiency of the response.

The knowledge and information gained during the short- and mid-term periods of the response and restoration should be used for the long-term planning of reinforcing the system before the next disaster. In addition, this rebuilding period should be used to bring the system to higher levels of robustness than before the disaster occurred.

Each disaster period requires quantitative metrics to assess the cost-benefit analysis for preparation and response. Cost-benefit analysis is difficult to make in the case of disasters. First, there is the cost of human lives, which is very difficult to quantify in economic terms. The cost of infrastructure recovery can be quantified in terms of direct repair and replacement costs. In addition to life and property, quantifying the costs should include the loss of quality of life until the system recovers a certain level of functionality. In the case of some disasters (e.g., wildfires or floods), there is also the long-term cost of environmental damage.

Sophisticated simulation tools exist today that can make use of the new advanced technologies to make more informed and effective decisions in emergency environments. A typical workflow for the use of these tools is as follows. First, predict the evolution of the disaster from the physics of the phenomenon and sensor measurements. Second, predict the damage expected to be caused by the advancing disaster. Third, play out what-if scenarios with possible responder actions and choose the action that will result in the best possible outcome.

Advanced prediction and optimized management tools can greatly reduce the consequences of loss of human lives and property. These advanced modelling and response tools can be used at all stages of the disaster, from reinforcing the system before the disaster by performing what-if scenarios and identifying the vulnerabilities to restoring the infrastructure in the shortest amount of time.

The chapters in this book present strategies for responding to natural disasters and using available technological and simulation advances to minimize their consequences.

Antonio Di Pietro,
Energy Technologies and Renewable Sources Department,
ENEA Casaccia Research Centre,
Rome, Italy

Josè Martì,
Department of Electrical and Computer Engineering,
The University of British Columbia,
Vancouver, Canada

Section 1

Introduction

Chapter 1

Introductory Chapter: Critical Infrastructure – Modern Approach and New Developments

Antonio Di Pietro and Josè Martì

1. Introduction

Disaster Risk Reduction aims at decreasing the damage caused by natural hazards, such as earthquakes, floods, droughts, and landslides, by implementing prevention and response measures. According to a 2022 report [1], 80% of cities have been affected by significant climate change hazards represented by extreme heat (46%), heavy rainfall (36%), drought (35%), and floods (33%). This set of hazards affects the complex system of the built environment and results in interrelated consequences at different scales ranging from single buildings to urban spaces and territorial infrastructures. Since it is not possible to reduce the severity of natural hazards, the main opportunity for lowering risk lies in reducing vulnerability and exposure. Vulnerability and exposure are related to urban development choices and practices that weaken the system's robustness. This volume reviews recent insights from risk identification and reduction to preparedness and financial protection strategies and proposes new approaches for better critical infrastructures and built environment protection.

Global warming and natural disasters are becoming more frequent and devastating to life and infrastructures. There are two types of natural disasters: uncontrollable and controllable. Uncontrollable disasters include earthquakes, tsunamis, windstorms, hurricanes, and others, for which the event's evolution is determined by nature, and when the disaster strikes, our responses are limited to early warning and repair actions. Controllable disasters are those like wildfires, floods, and pandemics, for which, in addition to early warning and repair actions, we can also modify the evolution of the event (e.g., wildfires, pandemics).

In addition to natural disasters becoming more prevalent, Critical Infrastructure and Systems are becoming increasingly interconnected, and the need to design for robustness and resiliency against man-made and natural threats has become a critical problem in our society [2]. An example of interdependent systems includes the electrical system that supplies the telecommunication system, which allows the mobile transmission, stoplights, light detectors, and railways that compose the modern transportation sector. If the electricity supply is not available, then the operations of these other systems will also be impacted.

2. System resilience

Although there are several definitions of resilience, we could define resilience as the capacity of a system to anticipate critical events and maintain operations during and recover from these events. In engineering literature, resilience plays a decisive role in studying critical infrastructure systems. However, most research regarding the resilience of critical infrastructure systems focuses on single, isolated systems, such as the electric grid, transportation, or water, without consideration of surrounding systems. Since Critical infrastructures are interdependent, these models fail to ensure the resilience of specific systems.

Based on the definition above, to strengthen resilience, it is necessary to improve the risk culture and strengthen the integration of resilience in the strategy process. Risk management includes five pillars: preparedness, mitigation, response, recovery, and evaluation. Preparedness refers to planning, training personnel, and providing educational activities regarding potentially disastrous events. Mitigation refers to actions to prevent or reduce the disasters' cause, impact, and consequences. The response phase occurs in the immediate aftermath of a disaster. When a disaster occurs, actions are taken to save lives, treat injuries, and minimize the effect of the disaster. During the recovery period, restoration efforts occur concurrently with regular operations and activities. Finally, evaluation includes actions to review the response effectiveness and reactions.

Technology, modelling, and simulation techniques can play a large role in analyzing resilience and estimating risk, and then implementing actions capable of lessening the consequences of disruptive events on lives and property. Regardless of the type of disaster, the timeline of a disaster can be divided into three periods: pre-disaster (preparedness and mitigation), during the disaster (response and recovery), and post-disaster (evaluation).

Figure 1 [3] shows the various stages involved in recovering a system damaged by a disaster, from preparation to recovery. The post-disaster period can be divided into immediately after a disaster, days after, weeks after, and months after. As shown in **Figure 1**, much effort should be put into the response immediately after the disaster

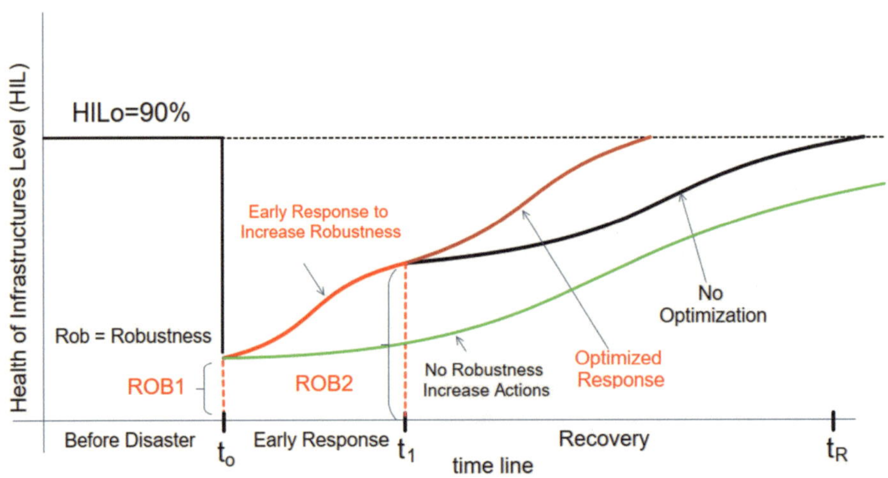

Figure 1.
Time stages of resilience.

(where most lives are at stake) and in optimizing the response in the early stages. Reinforcement of the system before the disaster happens increases the robustness of citizens and infrastructures. Reinforcement includes the preparation of the citizens in how to protect their lives during the event, reinforcement of buildings and homes, and reinforcement of the critical infrastructures (CIs). Similarly, being ready to increase robustness immediately after the disaster strikes has a strong influence on the overall consequences of the disaster. The decisions on prioritizing the assets to be reinforced more for a given CI budget will depend on the role of that asset in preventing loss of life and restoring the quality of life after the disaster.

A targeted and prioritized response as early as possible after the disaster (optimized response curve in **Figure 1**) requires knowing where the victims are located, the severity of their injuries, the transportation time, and the availability of treatment in the hospitals. The subsequent short-term and mid-term periods after the disaster focus on recovering infrastructure to restore people's well-being to a minimum level. The actions during the first days after the disaster will considerably impact the total time until a minimum functionality of the system is achieved. This period can be shortened from several weeks to a few days by increasing the efficiency of the response.

3. Preparation for the next disaster

The knowledge and information gained during the short- and mid-term periods of the response and restoration of a disaster should be used for the long-term planning of reinforcing the system before the next disaster. In addition, this rebuilding period should be used to bring the system to higher levels of robustness than before the previous disaster occurred.

Each disaster period requires quantitative metrics to assess the cost-benefit analysis for preparation and response. Cost-benefit analysis is difficult to make in the case of disasters. First, there is the cost of human lives, which is very difficult to quantify in economic terms. The cost of infrastructure recovery can be quantified in terms of direct repair and replacement costs. In addition to life and property, the quantification of the costs should include the loss of quality of life until the system recovers a certain level of functionality. In the case of some disasters (e.g., wildfires or floods), there is also the long-term cost of damage to the environment.

Sophisticated simulation tools exist today that can make use of the new advanced technologies to make more informed and effective decisions in emergency environments. A typical workflow for the use of these tools is as follows. First, predict the evolution of the disaster from the physics of the phenomenon and sensor measurements. Second, predict the damage expected to be caused by the advancing disaster. Third, play What-if scenarios with possible responder actions and choose the action that will result in the best possible outcome.

Advanced prediction and optimized management tools can greatly reduce the consequences of loss of human lives and property. These advanced modelling and response tools can be used at all stages of the disaster, from reinforcing the system before the disaster by performing what-if scenarios and identifying the vulnerabilities to restoring the infrastructure in the shortest amount of time.

The Chapters in this book present strategies for responding to natural disasters and making use of available technological and simulation advances to minimize their consequences.

Author details

Antonio Di Pietro[1*] and Josè Martì[2]

1 ENEA, National Agency for New Technologies, Energy and Sustainable Economic Development, Rome, Italy

2 Electrical and Computer Engineering, The University of British Columbia, Vancouver, BC, Canada

*Address all correspondence to: antonio.dipietro@enea.it

IntechOpen

© 2023 The Author(s). Licensee IntechOpen. This chapter is distributed under the terms of the Creative Commons Attribution License (http://creativecommons.org/licenses/by/3.0), which permits unrestricted use, distribution, and reproduction in any medium, provided the original work is properly cited.

References

[1] CDP. Protecting People and the Planet. Disclosure Insight Action. 2022

[2] Van Eeten M, Nieuwenhuijs A, Luiijf E, Klaver M, Cruz E. The state and the threat of cascading failure across critical infrastructures: The implications of empirical evidence from media incident reports. Public Administration. 2011;**89**:381-400. DOI: 10.1111/j.1467-9299.2011.01926.x

[3] Yang Z, Martí JR. Real-time resilience optimization combining an AI agent with online hard optimization. IEEE Transactions on Power Systems. 2021;**37**(1):508-517

Section 2

Analysis of Critical Infrastructures: Risk Identification and Reduction

Chapter 2

Resilience of Infrastructures and Systems to Multiple Hazardous Events: Application Cases and Future Perspectives

Clemente Fuggini, Miltiadis Kontogeorgos, Saimir Osmani and Fabio Bolletta

Abstract

Nowadays, Critical Infrastructure and Systems are getting more and more interconnected, while facing increasing and more intensive hazards: from man-made to natural ones, including those exacerbated by effects of the climate change. The demand for their robustness and resiliency against all these threats is finding ground to organizations' or states' ambitions and policies. The paper focuses on a review from an engineering perspective of past efforts and more importantly provides evidence of application cases the authors have developed in the past years. Finally, an outlook on future perspectives and potentials in the application of resilience is provided.

Keywords: resilience, hazards, complex systems, applications, impact assessment

1. Introduction

In today's landscape and emerging world, the significance of the Infrastructures and Systems (from Energy to Transportation ones) is becoming more and more critical for the well-tempered function of the states and communities. The increased demands in cities' energy consumption, the ever-expanding Transportation and Energy grids, the interconnection of these Systems and Infrastructures are some exemplary issues of this high criticality. In addition to these, the natural hazards due to climate change are appearing of higher magnitude and are causing more severe damages, estimating to billions of dollars worldwide annually [1], while future projections are predicting an increase of these costs the forthcoming years and decades [2–4]. Although the macroeconomic costs of the impacts due to climate change are highly uncertain, it is very likely to threaten development in many countries [5]. In addition, the man-made threats are always present for the global community, even expanding, due to terrorism, cyber-crime, and wars.

Under this prism, states and communities have already started to develop and set in force frameworks for robustness of their Infrastructures and Systems, both for their internal cohesion and uninterrupted continuity and for the more efficient co-operation among them in the international level. In the global sphere, cornerstones of global frameworks can be considered the Paris agreement [6] and the Sendai framework [7]. The Paris agreement is aiming to avoid more extreme natural phenomena and dangerous consequences due to climate change by taking measures in favor of global average temperature reduction, but also by enhancing societies' and states' capability to reduce the impacts of climate change. The Sendai framework has set up the priorities for actions for an effective disaster risk reduction and a resilient approach to these common threats, by understanding the disaster risk management to the enhancement of the disaster preparedness for effective response [7]. Furthermore, states or unions of countries (e.g., EU) have also developed their own frameworks [8–11], aligning simultaneously with the international agreements and goals, and showing special providence to cyber-resilience [12, 13].

The scientific and research community has faced the challenges and the demands for empowering the resiliency of Infrastructures and Systems. This was achieved by investigating many aspects of the resiliency planning against various hazards and developing in a scientific manner respective assessment and enhancement frameworks and tools. After the resilience conceptualization in a qualitative form, various quantitative metrics and approaches are suggested. Quantitative methods for assessing the resilience of Infrastructure Systems were proposed from many authors [14–16], also considering the interdependency of the Infrastructure Systems [17, 18] and expanding the field of study to the level of the communities [19]. Novel methodologies for analyzing Critical Infrastructure resilience were presented, with pilot implementation cases included as experimental part also [20]. As it was expected, studies were conducted also for examining the resilience capacity against specific hazards such as earthquake [21] or hurricane [22]. A special interest was shown for the resilience enhancement of Transport and Energy Infrastructures, due to their critical and multilevel meaning for the states' vitality and function.

The resilience of the Urban Transportation System was of interest for many researchers, and so many assessment methods were proposed [23, 24], including also multi-dimensional approach [25] and individual vertex-based and edge-based failure models [26]. The research has expanded beyond the Urban Transportation Systems, including also Railway [27, 28] and common Road and Transportation Systems [29, 30]. The factor of security has been highlighted, especially toward terrorism [31]. The Transportation Infrastructures and Systems have been tested also against various hazards, such as earthquake [32], extreme climatic and weather events [33, 34], and tsunami [35].

The vulnerability of Energy Infrastructures and Power Systems mainly to natural disasters due to climate change, but also due to manmade hazards, led the scientific community to develop assessment methods and solutions to increase the resilience capacity of these Systems. Frameworks and methods for the characterization of the resilience level of various types of Energy Infrastructures systems were proposed, such as for Nuclear Plants [36] and Hydrogen Systems [37]. Energy and Power Systems have been tested for their resilience capacity against various types of hazards such as hurricane [38], earthquake [39], or flooding [40]. In recent years, the resilience of the Energy Grids in the operational level [41], toward natural [42] or cyber [43] hazards, is being investigated thoroughly.

Although the multi-step progression in the definition of resiliency frameworks and the development of robustness' methods, Infrastructures and Systems are presenting a partial lack of efficient toolkits against multiple extreme events. Moreover, the cyber hazards are becoming more numerous and dangerous within the operational phase of the Systems, and the convergence of safety and cybersecurity has not been incorporated yet within the policies and the frameworks, which these Systems are following for their protection.

2. Methodology

A crucial element for the design of an efficient resiliency planning for Infrastructures and Systems, aiming at their protection toward multiple hazardous events, is the adopted methodology. Due to the flexibility that demands in order to be feasible for implementation to various assets and against various hazards, the methodology is setting some standard steps toward the resilience design, and then it is focusing partially on the specific asset and threat for every case. The procedure followed is being described in the **Figure 1**.

The initial step refers to the description and the characterization of the entire System (i.e., Energy System, Healthcare system), including all the necessary information, which is needed in the resiliency analysis. These can be the placement of the System toward the external environment and the interdependency between the System's elements or assets.

The next phase contains the asset characterization. This step refers more to technical information for the asset of our interest. For example, if the resilience planning aims at Energy Infrastructures, the characterization is needed to include the type of the Infrastructure (i.e., gas transmission pipeline, refineries, power plants) and then the design details and the qualifying characteristics. In case of a bridge asset, it needed the type of bridge (i.e., suspended) and the design details of the project (i.e., type of foundation, reinforcement blueprints), and so forth, regarding every asset under resilience evaluation.

The third step is about the threat characterization. The identification of potential threats and hazards is carried out, after the evaluation of the disruptive event's magnitude and criticality, and the definition of relevant hazard scenarios is taking place. According to the examined hazards, a modeling of them is following, respecting the literature database and the national codes and frameworks. In this step are included calculations such as the creation of probabilistic seismic curves due to site characteristics or the probabilistic scenarios for landslides and floodings based on site and meteorological data available.

The first three steps were decided more as part of constructing the profile of the interested Infrastructure or System and then defining the problem. The fourth and fifth steps are closer to final goal of the methodology, and they are the core of the followed philosophy. So, the fourth step is devoted to the risk and vulnerability assessment, along with the impact analysis. A quantitative expression based on failure probabilities for the examined Infrastructure or System is conducted, under the form of a vulnerability curve. This step is connecting the existing situation and behavior of the asset toward multiple scenarios of the hazards' magnitude, by defining the failure limits of the asset. Furthermore, regarding the magnitude and the intensity of an event beyond the capacity's limits, an impact analysis is conducted. The impact analysis takes into account the economic, social, environmental, and human losses aspects of a disruptive event and determines the total direct and indirect losses caused to the stakeholders (i.e., energy operators, civil protection, state) and the society. Again, the analysis contains some general criteria and aspects covered, but is delving also into specific impact details and information, respectively, to the type of the asset.

Figure 1.
Schematic representation of the methodology's philosophy.

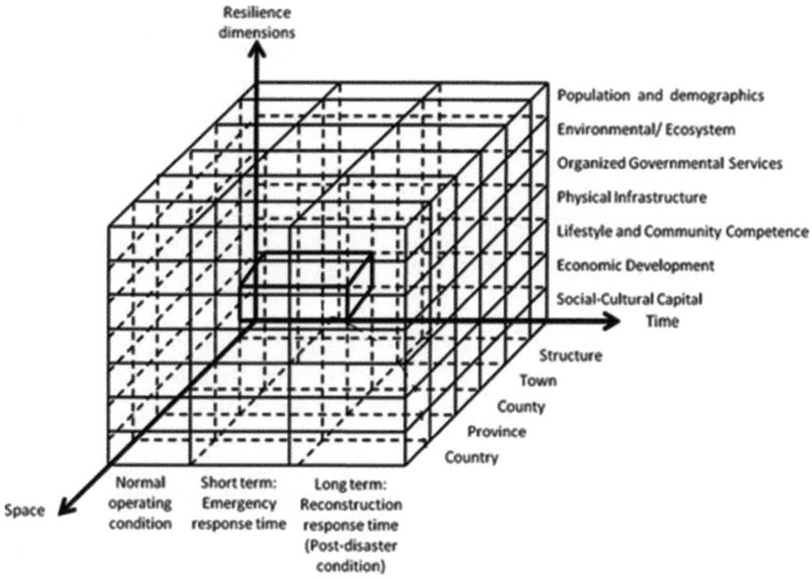

Figure 2.
Depiction of the resilience dimensions, in terms of space, time, and type of resilience analysis.

The last and final step is including the desirable resilience assessment. After the processing of all the necessary information toward the asset and the investigated threats, the level of service and the resilience capacity are defined. These are expressed in a quantitative form, as for this step, a set of various resilience indicators and a resilience matrix have been developed and exploited. The resilience matrix contains the robustness, rapidity, resourcefulness, redundancy sections, and after the evaluation on these specific domains, a grading of the behavior and response of the asset or the system is calculated toward a unique or multiple hazardous events.

The range of applications for a methodological approach of this type, in terms of time, space, and aspects of resilience assessment, is depicted briefly in the **Figure 2**. The analysis can be targeted to examine the operational phase of an Infrastructure or System, but also the emergency and post-recovery phase after a disruptive event. The space covered and examined in the resilience analysis can begin from a single building/structure (i.e., cultural heritage building toward seismic hazard) and extend to a whole province or country (i.e., the national gas transmission or transport network). Finally, the aspects of resilience analysis that will contribute to the calculation of the total resilience capacity can include the social or the environmental factor, except those for the technical level of the System and the economic depiction of a disruptive event.

3. Application cases

The applications that are presented by the authors are selected in order to cover both Transportation Systems' and Energy Infrastructures' fields, by implementing the before-mentioned methodology approach and describing promising technologies for the increase of the resilience. The applications are derived or inspired from EU-funded projects. More specifically, the chosen application as an exemplary case for the Transportation Systems is describing the FORESEE project. This application is focusing on short- and long-term resilience schemes for rail and road corridors and logistics terminals. The Energy Infrastructure case is depicting the SecureGas project, which is dealing with the strengthening of the security and resilience of the European Gas Network, regarding the physical and cyber threats. Finally, the presentation of the INSPIRE project serves as an introduction to the beneficial use of potential meta-materials concepts within Infrastructures (especially Energy) and Systems, regarding their protection toward dynamic-nature hazards.

3.1 Transportation system

The main goal of the FORESEE application was to provide road authorities and managers, responsible for the rail and road corridors and logistics terminals, with a solution to anticipate, absorb, adapt, and rapidly recover from a potentially disruptive hazard or extreme event during the entire lifecycle of the transport infrastructure: planning, design, construction, operation, and maintenance [44]. In order to achieve this goal, the proposed methodology is implemented in all its five steps, and a toolkit, which is capable of collecting data for predicting the magnitude and the potential damage of various hazards to the asset of our interest, has been developed for that reason. The whole structure of the toolkit, which is aligned with the authors' methodological approach, is presented schematically in **Figure 3**.

3.1.1 System characterization

The first step is the system characterization. A whole Transportation System's network description is being conducted, also including its key elements, which are the bridges and the tunnels. Moreover, demand data (i.e., N° of vehicles/hour, traffic flow intensity, driving directions) are being collected from every available source and are being exploited as input data for the toolkit.

3.1.2 Asset characterization

In this phase, the asset characterization is focused on the network components (here bridges, tunnels, and road). The components' description is including the asset's

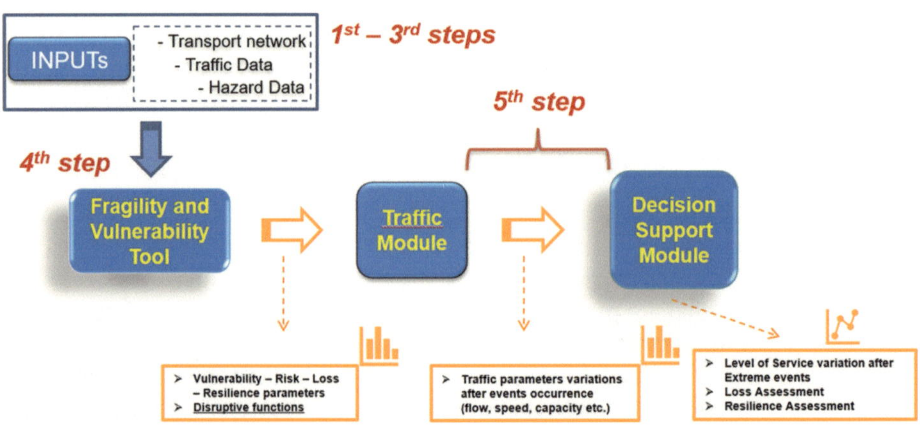

Figure 3.
Schematic representation of the toolkit's design philosophy, aligning with the followed methodology's steps.

main properties, mainly the technical details and the design data of the structures (e.g., N° of bridges' piers, deck length). The site conditions (e.g., soil properties, slopes characteristics) are taken also into consideration as they are very important data for the behavior of the asset and the hazard characterization.

3.1.3 Threat characterization

The third step is the hazard definition and evaluation. For this step, every resource available in literature, web sources, or data shared from the infrastructure's managers are being exploited. And one of the novelties is that the toolkit can integrate satellite and terrestrial data in the analysis and the assessment of the hazards. This way, the desirable data-driven diagnostic framework is strengthened sufficiently from the accuracy of the data input. It follows a definition of relevant hazard scenarios and relevant hazard modeling (e.g., seismic and rainfall curves) in the area considered.

3.1.4 Risk, vulnerability, and impact

The before-mentioned step is necessary for the calculation of the fragility (**Figure 4**) and restoration functions, along with the vulnerability curves, toward the investigated hazard. The fragility functions can be derived from methodologies, which are found to the existing databases or literature, or from a more targeted and accurate analysis, from the Finite Element modeling. The followed impact analysis consists of the operativity loss, risk quantification, loss curves, and expected annual loss. In this step, it is important, especially for the System's operators, the calculation of the Expected Annual Loss (EAL), as part of the impact analysis. It provides the annual loss of the asset, as percentage of the repair cost, for a given hazard. These losses are generated by the repair costs applied to the asset after a possible hazard occurrence.

3.1.5 Resilience assessment

The integration of all this information is leading to the creation of the multi-scenarios in which the Transportation System will be simulated, and the final resilience assessment will be conducted, under a specific framework with indicators and

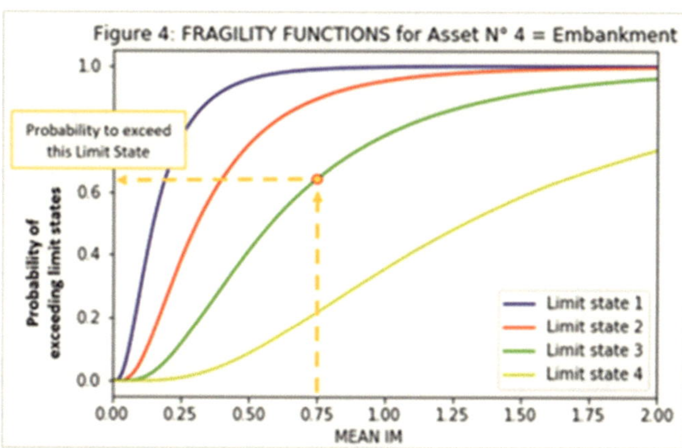

Figure 4.
Typical fragility function (e.g., for earthquake).

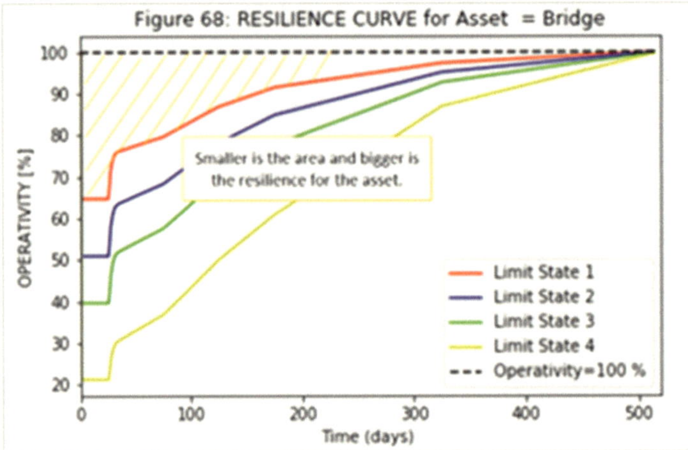

Figure 5.
Typical results presented for a resilience assessment of an asset (e.g., bridge).

different assumptions (i.e., deterministic or indeterministic approaches). The results are expressed in terms of operativity and time for the various limit states of the asset (**Figure 5**). The final goal of the resilience assessment is the creation of the necessary input for decision support tool, which is an instrument offered to Infrastructure managers about disruptive hazards impacting effects on their assets, and it enhances the overall operational phase of the Systems and Infrastructures.

3.2 Energy infrastructure

The application of the SecureGas was aiming more to a resilience design and management (**Figure 6**), rather than to a resilience assessment or risk management, of a gas transmission network. The methodology is adjusted respectively to the outer goal and this way, the desired adaptability is being justified in practice. The first three steps of the methodological approach are the same, and the subsequent upgrade of the overall resilient behavior was considered granted.

3.2.1 System characterization

In this initial step, the system characterization follows this of a typical gas network and plants, which means that special focus was given to the location (site characteristics), geo-politics, and climate. The first step was closely connected to the threat characterization, as the hazards were taken into consideration after the study of the relevance literature for the respective system characterization for a gas transmission network.

3.2.2 Asset characterization

Every technical and design details were collected in this phase, especially those referring to the safety and the security of the gas plants and networks operational phase (e.g., maximum gas pressure in the pipelines). Every step on the gas value chain was taken into consideration (production, storage, transmission, distribution), and the safety protocols were followed in detail.

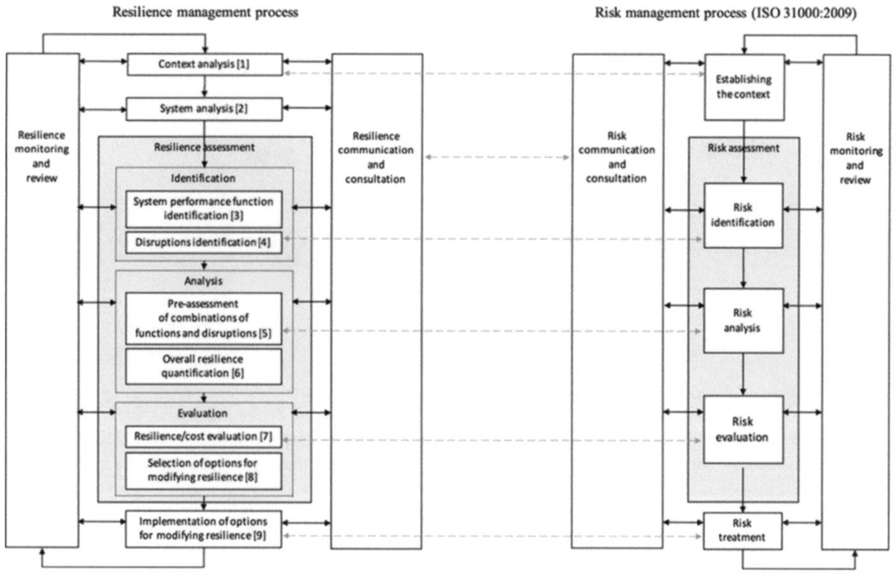

Figure 6.
A typical flowchart of resilience management process, which is aligned with the proposed methodology, as it has incorporated its basic steps and the final resilience assessment/quantification, also including the risk management of an asset and the monitoring of the resilience behavior.

3.2.3 Threat characterization

The threat characterization was conducted based on the literature, searching for the most frequently classified threats, and the user requirements, which have been set with by the end-users, in order to align better with their needs in the real-life circle of the assets' operational function [45]. Among them are the external interference or third-party activity (including political/geo-political interference), corrosion, construction defect and mechanical or material failure, natural hazards, operational error, and cyber-attacks [46].

3.2.4 Resilience management

The fourth and fifth steps here can be considered as the resilient design, which is shifting to the operational management of the Infrastructure, and not only the assessment phase. So, within SecureGas project, a toolkit based on High-Level Architecture [46] and the respective Conceptual Model followed was developed, aiming at the prevention, detection, response, and mitigation of combined physical and cyber threats to gas transmission grid network. Following this philosophy as an expansion of the proposed methodology, the resilience management of the asset (**Figure 7**) is enhancing and has become more robust toward any potential threat and hazards identified in the second step.

The main goal and the novelty of this toolkit is the convergence between physical and cyber threats or the so-called safety-security convergence. A central and undivided platform was designed, which covers the user requirements and where all the threats (cyber, natural, and man-made) to the gas transmission network or the plant can be addressed and recorded. The input data are derived from the sensors placed to the network and the plant, the UAV inspecting the facilities and the software for the cyber-protection of the System's operation.

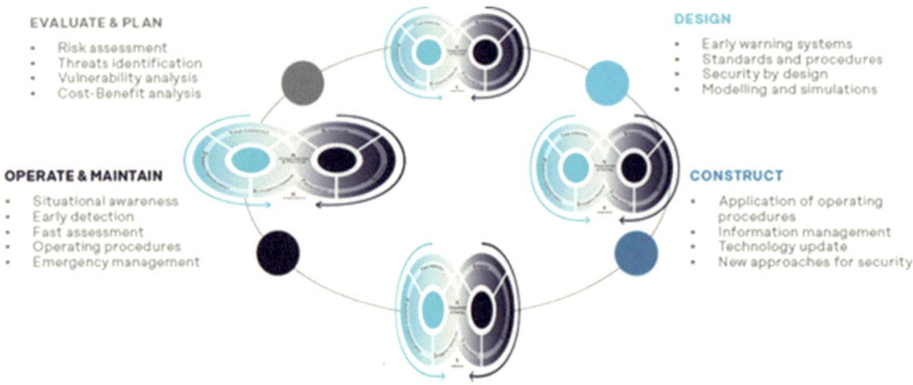

Figure 7.
Brief representation of the resilience management process across the life cycle of an infrastructure followed from RINA, where the proposed methodology is contributing to the design and evaluate and plan phase (source: RINA).

This way, the surveillance and the control of the asset in the operational level are becoming more efficient, and the grid is enhancing its safety against multiple hazards. The real-time monitoring of the grid's condition is securing the high level of the situational awareness, and the early detection of disruptive event is leading to faster restoration of potential damage and a more targeted emergency management. The decision support system is based on the data acquisition and the threat evaluation, while the feature for the information sharing with the public is securing the safety of the communities.

3.3 Meta-materials and energy infrastructures

The notion of "meta-materials" refers to natural or artificial materials or structures, which exhibit extraordinary properties for inhibiting or conditioning wave propagation in all spatial directions over broad frequency bands [47], and this way, protecting the underlying structures toward dynamic-nature hazards. Due to the periodic structure of the meta-materials, the so-called band-gaps are being created, which are considered to be mitigation zones for specific frequency ranges of the transmitted waves (**Figure 8**). This way, the potential damage from dynamic-nature phenomena such as blast or seismic is mitigated, or in some cases, the structures are becoming isolated toward this hazard.

Meta-materials are relatively recent to the civil engineering design practices, but concepts based on this design philosophy for the protection of Energy Infrastructures have been already developed. Examples of them are the seismic protection of fuel storage tanks [48] and of nuclear plants [49] via the concept of a meta-foundation. Also, a meta-material concept for the blast protection of gas transmission pipelines has been proposed [50], and it is shown in **Figure 9**. It is worth noted that the already existing meta-material concepts such as the meta-concrete [51] or the meta-barriers [52] can be implemented for the increase of the resilience capacity of Energy Infrastructures and Transportation Systems, but the beneficial implementation of them has not yet been evaluated. Finally, meta-materials concepts can be exploited for the enhancing the resilience level of already constructed Energy Infrastructures, as they can be placed around the structure.

The comparative advantage of the meta-materials is the upgrade of the resilience capacity from the design phase of a civil engineering project. Although, there are

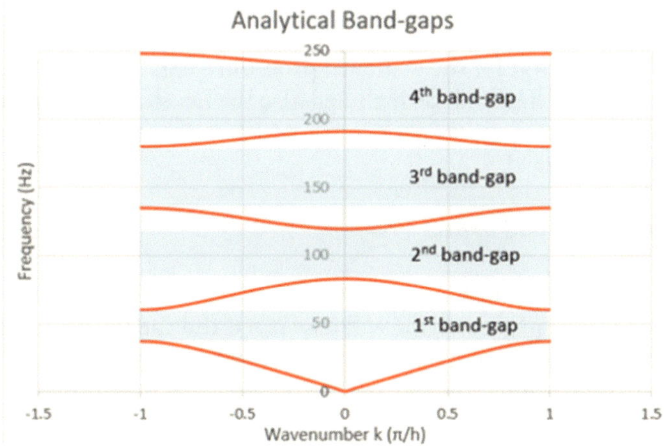

Figure 8.
A typical example of a band-gap, expressed in terms of frequency and length wavenumber, where the shaded regions are considered the mitigation zones for transmitting waves of these frequency ranges.

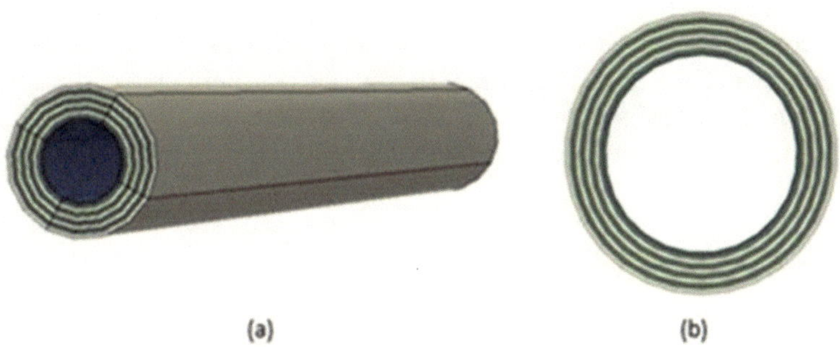

Figure 9.
The proposed meta-material concept for the protection of gas transmission pipelines, in a) exploded view and b) cross section [50]. The successive layers of the two different materials are leading to the creation of the band-gaps and the zones of energy mitigation.

solutions of this philosophy (e.g., meta-barriers) that can be exploited in order to reinforce the behavior of the System or a specific Infrastructure toward specific hazards. For both cases, the methodological approach can still be implemented and lead to a comparative study of the resilience level between solutions, which are including or not the existence of meta-materials in their scope.

3.3.1 System characterization

Regarding the type of the Energy Infrastructures, the system characterization will follow the standard procedure of collecting the necessary data and information.

3.3.2 Asset characterization

Regarding the type of the Energy Infrastructures, the system characterization will follow the standard procedure of collecting the necessary data and information.

3.3.3 Threat characterization

In the third step, except for the standard procedure regarding the type of the Energy Infrastructure, there will be included also the necessary information for the respective design of a meta-material concept, which means the frequency spectra of the dynamic-nature hazard.

3.3.4 Risk, vulnerability, and impact

Toward the fourth and most crucial step, the calculation of the vulnerability and risk assessment for the specific threat will take place and the results for the solution based on the meta-materials will reveal the beneficial presence of these concepts to the respective damage mitigation and risk reduction.

3.3.5 Resilience assessment

The subsequent enhancement of the resilience capacity will be verified, in the fifth and last step, following the before-mentioned resiliency framework and metrics.

In this case, the methodological approach is contributing, especially via the comparative calculation of the vulnerabilities and the impact analyses, to the highlighting of these meta-material-based solutions for the scope of the Infrastructures' and Systems' resilience. Under a more general prism, a way is being paved for respective advanced methods of design, which are derived from the latest research achievements, to be transferred in the real-world projects, serving the goal of resilience.

4. Future perspectives

The further expansion of the current knowledge is crucial, and it is needed to be oriented in the future demands and landscape of Infrastructures and Systems. The proposed resilience methodology and the respective application cases that were presented are future-oriented, but their future exploitation is not limited to the so far produced results. For this reason, the authors are giving directions and are suggesting potential concepts, based on the investigated fields of interest.

4.1 Transportation systems

The methodological resilience assessment process, which was followed in the Transportation System's application, and the toolkit, which led to a decision support system, are needed to be expanded in other types of Infrastructures, such as these in the sector of Energy. Also, the current range of applications can include the resilience assessment of Transportation Systems during war or the so-called war resilience assessment. The authors' suggestions are being presented in **Table 1**.

4.2 Energy infrastructures

The Gas Energy Infrastructure's toolkit has spotlighted the significance of the convergence between physical and cyber security and the subsequent upgrade of the resilience capacity for the gas network grid. It is needed also to expand its feasibility for tackling hybrid threats and warfare. Furthermore, the whole function and the

Type of infrastructure or system	Hazard
Transportation Systems	Expand the existing resilience assessment methodology of the Transportation Systems to the war resilience field
Energy Infrastructure	Expand the existing resilience assessment method to the Energy Infrastructures (including power plants and transmission grids)

Table 1.
Authors' suggestions for future exploitation of Transportation System's application.

Type of infrastructure or system	Hazard
Gas Network	Upgrade the existing resilience toolkit for facing the hybrid threats and the subsequent hybrid warfare
Energy Infrastructure	Expand the existing resilience toolkit to other types of Energy Infrastructures (including electricity and hydrogen power plants)

Table 2.
Authors' suggestion for future exploitation of the Energy Infrastructure's application.

Type of infrastructure	Hazard
Gas Transmission Pipelines	Surface & Underground Explosion
Underwater Transmission Pipelines	Underwater Explosion
Offshore Wind Turbine	Underwater Explosion
Electricity Plants	Seismic Protection
Geothermal Energy Plants	Seismic Protection

Table 3.
Authors' suggestion for future exploitation of meta-materials concepts for the resilience upgrade of Energy Infrastructures.

capabilities of the specific solution (indicated by the proposed methodology) can inspire respective toolkits for other types of energy plants or transmission grids. The authors' suggestions are being presented in **Table 2**.

In the field of advanced materials' exploitation for the scope of the resilience enhancement, the future perspectives and the range of applications are more. Various meta-material concepts can be exploited for the purposes of upgrading the resilience profile of existing or new Energy Infrastructures. They can also be implemented to numerous types of Energy Infrastructures such as electricity plants or underwater pipeline grid, against various types of hazards such as blast or seismic. The authors' suggestions are being presented in **Table 3**.

5. Conclusion

The aim of this study was to demonstrate novel approaches for the enhancement of the resilience for the Infrastructures and Systems, via a specific methodological approach, which has been followed within three applications, mainly cases referred to

Transport Systems and Energy Infrastructures. The promising and efficient methodological approach is clearly presented in its general structure and then was specified for every project. The application cases were chosen in order to spotlight the need for upgrade in the design philosophy for the resiliency planning and the robustness methods, regarding the current and future demands. A powerful toolkit is developed in order the methodological approach to be followed in the technical level, in scope of Transport Systems' resilience assessment. The convergence of safety and cyber-security is of high importance for the Infrastructures and Systems resilience management, and it is needed to be considered in every approach for the robustness of a resilience planning. Advanced technologies such as meta-materials can upgrade the resilience capacity of various projects (e.g., Energy Infrastructures) even from the design phase, and it paved a way in order the research-based technical solution to be integrated in resiliency frameworks. The authors have also described the future perspectives of the methodology in the studied sections and suggested specific concepts and directions for the further exploitation.

Acknowledgements

The authors acknowledge the financial support from the European Commission, as the INSPIRE project has received funding from the European Union's Horizon 2020 research and innovation program under the Marie Skłodowska-Curie grant agreement No. 813424, the SecureGas project has received funding from the European Union's Horizon 2020 research and innovation program under the grant agreement No. 833017, and the FORESEE project has received funding from the European Union's Horizon 2020 research and innovation program under the grant agreement No. 769373.

Conflict of interest

The authors declare no conflict of interest.

Notes

Due to confidentiality reasons, it was not allowed to share specific results and values in some of the application presented. Whoever will be interested into more details about the applications can contact the author for further questions.

Author details

Clemente Fuggini[1], Miltiadis Kontogeorgos[1,2]*, Saimir Osmani[1] and Fabio Bolletta[1]

1 Rina Consulting S.p.A., Rozzano, Italy

2 School of Civil Engineering, National Technical University of Athens, Athens, Greece

*Address all correspondence to: miltiadis.kontogeorgos@rina.org

IntechOpen

© 2022 The Author(s). Licensee IntechOpen. This chapter is distributed under the terms of the Creative Commons Attribution License (http://creativecommons.org/licenses/by/3.0), which permits unrestricted use, distribution, and reproduction in any medium, provided the original work is properly cited.

References

[1] Hallegatte S, Rentschler J, Julie R. Lifelines: The Resilient Infrastructure Opportunity. Washington: World Bank; 2019

[2] Neumann JE, Price J, Chinowsky P, Wright L, Ludwig L, Streeter R, et al. Climate change risks to US infrastructure: Impacts on roads, bridges, coastal development, and urban drainage. Climatic Change. 2015;**131**(1):97-109

[3] Shiklomanov N, Streletskiy AD, Suter L. Assessment of the cost of climate change impacts on critical infrastructure in the circumpolar Arctic. Polar Geography 2019;**42**(12):1-20

[4] Twerefou KD, Chinowsky P, Adjei-Mantey K, Strzepek LK. The economic impact of climate change on road infrastructure in Ghana. Sustainability. 2015;7(9):11949-11966

[5] Abeygunawardena VP, Knill Y, Foy P, Harrold T, Steele M, Tanner P, et al. Poverty and Climate Change: Reducing the Vulnerability of the Poor through Adaptation. Washington: World Bank; 2009

[6] Paris Agreement 2015 of United Nations. 2015. Available from: https://unfccc.int/sites/default/files/english_paris_agreement.pdf [Accessed: August 14, 2022]

[7] Sendai Framework for Disaster Risk Reduction 2015-2030. 2015. Available from: https://www.preventionweb.net/files/44983_sendaiframeworkchart.pdf [Accessed: August 14, 2022]

[8] Disaster Resilience Framework: Principles for Analyzing Federal Efforts to Facilitate and Promote Resilience to Natural Disasters [Internet]. 2019. Available from: https://www.gao.gov/assets/gao-20-100sp.pdf [Accessed: August 14, 2022]

[9] Resilience Framework of U.S. Department of Homeland Security. 2018. Available from: https://www.dhs.gov/sites/default/files/publications/dhs_resilience_framework_july_2018_508.pdf [Accessed: August 14, 2022]

[10] Proposal for a DIRECTIVE OF THE EUROPEAN PARLIAMENT AND OF THE COUNCIL on the resilience of critical entities [Internet]. 2020. Available from: https://eur-lex.europa.eu/legal-content/EN/TXT/?uri=CELEX%3A52020PC0829 [Accessed: August 14, 2022]

[11] National Committee on Sustainable Development Goals. UAE and the 2030 agenda for Sustainable Development. Dubai: Federal Competitiveness & Statistics Authority Secretariat for UAE National Committee on SDGs; 2017

[12] Directive (EU) 2016/1148 of the European Parliament and of the Council of 6 July 2016 concerning measures for a high common level of security of network and information systems across the Union [Internet]. 2016. Available from: https://eur-lex.europa.eu/eli/dir/2016/1148/oj [Accessed: August 14, 2022]

[13] Framework for Improving Critical Infrastructure Cybersecurity from National Institute of Standards and Technology [Internet]. 2018. Available from: https://nvlpubs.nist.gov/nistpubs/CSWP/NIST.CSWP.04162018.pdf [Accessed: August 14, 2022]

[14] Didier M, Broccardo M, Esposito S, Stojadinovic B. A compositional demand/supply framework to quantify the

resilience of civil infrastructure systems (Re-CoDeS). Sustainable and Resilient Infrastructure. 2018;**3**(2):86-102

[15] Nan C, Sansavini G, Kröger W, Heinimann H. Quantitative methods for assessing the resilience of infrastructure systems. In: Probabilistic Safety Assessment and Management (PSAM '12). Honolulu. Hawaii; June 2014

[16] Ongkowijoyo CS, Doloi H. Risk-based resilience assessment model focusing on urban infrastructure system restoration. Procedia Engineering. 2018;**212**:1115-1122

[17] Kong J, Simonovic SP, Zhang C. Resilience assessment of interdependent infrastructure systems: A case study based on different response strategies. Sustainability. 2019;**11**(23):6552

[18] Liu X, Prodan I, Zio E. Resilience analysis of interconnected systems by a set-theoretic approach. In: Congres Lambda Mu 19. Dijon, France; 2014

[19] Blagojevic N, Didier M, Hefti F, Henken J, Stojadinovic B. Quantifying disaster resilience of a community with interdependent civil infrastructure systems. Structure and Infrastructure Engineering. 2022. Available from: https://www.tandfonline.com/action/showCitFormats?doi=10.1080%2F15732479.2022.2052912&area=0000000000000001. DOI: 10.1080/15732479.2022.2052912

[20] Storesund K, Reitan KN, Sjöström J, Rød B, Guay F, Almeida R, et al. Novel methodologies for analysing critical infrastructure resilience. In: Safety and Reliability – Safe Societies in a Changing World. Trondheim, Norway; 2014

[21] Shafieezadeh A, Burden I.V. Scenario-based resilience assessment framework for critical infrastructure systems: Case study for seismic resilience of seaports. Reliability Engineering & System Safety. 2014; 132: 207-219

[22] Tokgoz BE, Gheorghe AV. Resilience quantification and its application to a residential building subject to hurricane winds. International Journal of Disaster Risk Science. 2013;**4**(3):105-114

[23] Leobons CM, Gouvêa Campos VB, Bandeira M. Assessing urban transportation systems resilience: A proposal of indicators. Transportation Research Procedia. 2019;**37**:322-329

[24] Gonçalves JPAL, Riberio P. Resilience of urban transportation systems. Concept, characteristics, and methods. Journal of Transport Geography. 2020;**85**(11):102727

[25] Khagani F, Jazizadeh F. mD-resilience: A multi-dimensional approach for resilience-based performance assessment in urban transportation. Sustainability. 2020;**12**(12):4879

[26] Wang J, Gao Y. A resilience assessment framework for urban transportation systems. International Journal of Production Research. 2020;**59**(2):1-16

[27] Enache FM, Al-Janabi D, Letia T. Conceiving of resilient railway systems. In: International Conference on Automation, Quality and Testing, Robotics (AQTR). Cluj-Napoca, Romania; 2020

[28] Regt de A, Siegel WA, Schraagen MJ. Toward quantifying metrics for rail-system resilience: Identification and analysis of performance weak resilience signals. Cognition Technology and Work. 2016;**18**(2):319-331

[29] Leviäkangas P, Aapaoja A. Resilience of transport infrastructure

systems. CSID Journal of Infrastructure Development. 2015;**1**(1):80-90

[30] Do M, Jung H. Enhancing road network resilience by considering the performance loss and asset value. Sustainability. 2018;**10**(11):4188

[31] Cox A, Prager F, Rose A. Transportation security and the role of resilience: A Foundation for Operational Metrics. Transport Policy. 2011;**18**(2): 307-317

[32] Shafei B, Alipour A. Seismic resilience of transportation networks with deteriorating components. Journal of Structural Engineering. 2016;**142**(8):C4015015

[33] Testa AC, Furtado MN, Alipour A. Resilience of coastal transportation networks faced with extreme climatic events. Journal of the Transportation Research Board. 2015;**2532**(1)

[34] Valenzuela YB, Rosas SR, Mazari M, Risse M, Rodriguez-Nikl T. Resilience of road infrastructure in response to extreme weather events. In: International Conference on Sustainable Infrastructure. New York, USA; 2017

[35] van Dijk M. Tsunami Resiliency of Transport Systems [thesis]. Delft: Delft University of Technology; 2018

[36] Labaka L, Hernantes J, Sarriegi JM. Resilience framework for critical infrastructures: An empirical study in a nuclear plant. Reliability Engineering & System Safety. 2015;**141**:92-105

[37] Afgan N, Veziroglu A. Sustainable resilience of hydrogen energy system. International Journal of Hydrogen Energy. 2012;**37**:5461-5467

[38] Ouyang M, Dueñas-Osorio L. Multi-dimensional hurricane resilience assessment of electric power systems. Journal of Structural Safety. 2012;**48**:15-24

[39] Sun L, Stojadinovic B, Sansavini G. Resilience evaluation framework for integrated civil infrastructure-community systems under seismic hazard. In: 16th World Conference on Earthquake. Santiago, Chile; 2017

[40] Souto L, Yip J, Wu WJ, Austgen B, Kutanoglu E, Hasenbein J, et al. Power system resilience to floods: Modeling, impact assessment, and mid-term mitigation strategies. International Journal of Electrical Power & Energy Systems. 2022;**135**(3):107545. DOI: 10.1016/j.ijepes.2021.107545

[41] Cotilla-Sanchez E, Ekisheva S, Papic M. A risk-based approach to assess the operational resilience of transmission grids. Applied Sciences. 2020;**10**(14):4761

[42] Maccioni M, Bragatto T, Cresta M, Cortesi F, Gatta F, Geri A, et al. Assessment and possible solution to increase resilience: Flooding threats in Terni distribution grid. Energies. 2019;**12**(4):4761

[43] Nguyen T, Wang S, Alhazmi M, Nazemi M, Estebsari A, Dehghanian P. Electric power grid resilience to cyber adversaries: State of the art. IEEE Access. 2020;**2020**:8

[44] About the FORESEE project [Internet]. 2018. Available from: https://foreseeproject.eu/about-us/ [Accessed: August 14, 2022]

[45] Agrafioti E, Chalkidoy A, Papadakis G, Gazi A, Gkotsi I, Stritecku V, et al. The SecureGas Key Performance Indicators. In: Soldatos J, Praça I, Jovanovic A, editors. Cyber-Physical Threat Intelligence for Critical Infrastructures Security: Securing Critical Infrastructures in Air Transport, Water, Gas, Healthcare, Finance and Industry.

Boston-Delft: Now Publishers Inc; 2021. pp. 342-360

[46] SecureGas deliverable 2.2. 2021

[47] About the INSPIRE project [Internet]. 2018. Available from: https://itn-inspire.eu/about/ [Accessed: August 14, 2022]

[48] Bursi SO, Basone F, Wenzel M, Fossetti M. Finite locally resonant Meta-foundations for the seismic protection of fuel storage tanks. Earthquake Engineering & Structural Dynamics. 2018;**48**(2):232-252. DOI: 10.1002/eqe.3134

[49] Mo YL, Witarto W, Tang Y, Wang SJ, Yang CY, Chang KC, et al. Three-dimensional periodic materials as seismic base isolator for nuclear infrastructure. AIP Advances. 2019;**9**(4):045014

[50] Kontogeorgos M, Fuggini C. Meta-material layout for the protection of buried steel pipes against surface explosion. Geotechnics. 2022;**2**(2):427-440

[51] Pandolfi A, Ortiz M, Bricolla D. Experimental validation of Metaconcrete blast mitigation properties. Journal of Applied Mechanics. 2019;**84**:031001

[52] Palermo A, Krödel S, Marzani A, Daraio C. Engineered metabarrier as shield from seismic surface waves. Scientific Reports. 2016;**6**(1):39356

Chapter 3

An Open-Data-Based Methodology for the Creation of a Graph of Critical Infrastructure Dependencies at an Urban Scale

Antonio Di Pietro, Alessandro Calabrese,
Antonio De Nicola, Daniele Ferneti, Luisa Franchina,
Josè Martì and Tommaso Ruocco

Abstract

This paper presents the MARIS (*Modeling infrAstructuRe dependencIes at an urban Scale*) methodology, allowing the generalization of one of the possible graphs modeling Critical Infrastructure (CI, hereafter) interdependencies at an urban scale starting from uncertain data. This leverages a set of known interdependencies at the system level, topological open data of local services and Points of Interest collected at an urban scale, and some heuristics. Indeed, interdependencies at an urban scale are usually not known to decision makers (e.g., CI operators, emergency planners) due to, for example, a lack of integration of knowledge held by different critical infrastructure operators and privacy restrictions. Here, these interdependencies are determined through geographic-based strategies. The resulting graph can be a valuable input to simulate emergency scenarios of CIs in the area of interest and, thus, plan proper countermeasures.

Keywords: interdependencies, open-data, critical infrastructures, graph, GIS

1. Introduction

Nowadays, Critical Infrastructures (CI) (roads and railways, electrical and telecommunication networks, gas and water pipelines, etc.), supplying primary services to citizens, are mutually connected as they provide their services not only to final users but also to other infrastructures. In this aspect, infrastructures are said to be dependent on each other and" interdependent." The concept of dependency stands on the fact that an infrastructure (e.g., the electrical network) provides service to another (e.g., the telecommunication network), and, thus, the latter is said to be dependent on the former. CI interdependencies can involve different abstraction layers. For instance, a general statement about the dependency between a railway and a power station involves a different layer related to a railway and a power station located in a given city.

 IntechOpen

For the sake of simplicity, in the following, we refer to the former as *system dependency* and to the latter as *urban dependency*.

Whereas repositories of system dependencies already exist[1], these are not sufficient to build urban dependencies due to several factors including lack of integration of knowledge held by different critical infrastructure operators and privacy restrictions. Furthermore, these data are constantly changing and difficult to collect because different stakeholders keep them. In order to build simulation models, the unavailability of information on real interdependencies is generally overcome using literature data or through survey data analysis addressed to critical infrastructure experts [1]. However, interdependency data would allow more reliable simulation for risk assessment and crisis management in case of natural events, such as earthquakes, or other events, such as cyber-attacks.

In this context, this paper aims to define a methodology to generate one of the possible graphs modeling CI interdependencies at an urban scale starting from uncertain data. The proposed methodology, named MARIS (Modeling infrAstructuRe dependencIes at an urban Scale), allows the discover of possible hidden dependencies using Geographical Information System (GIS) Open data of CIs and Points of Interest (e.g., the location of substations of an electric distribution network serving an urban area) and to apply proximity criteria to model dependencies when these are not known.

In addition, the paper presents the results of a survey on CIs conducted by several experts from Italy, aiming at quantifying the dependencies between critical infrastructures. This can be a valuable input for applying the MARIS methodology to produce realistic graphs of interdependencies in an urban context.

The rest of the paper is organized as it follows. Section 2 gives an overview of the present work on CI interdependencies. Section 3 presents the MARIS methodology. Section 4 presents a survey analysis of experts on the dependencies between Critical Infrastructures. Section 5 describes a case study related to Rome in Italy. Finally, Section 6 concludes the paper.

2. Related work

Modeling of CI interdependencies has been considered as a relevant problem since the seminal paper of [2].

In Chiara et al. [3], the authors proposed the Mixed Holistic Reductionist (MHR) methodology based on the interaction of three layers: (i) a holistic layer where CIs are seen as singular entities with defined boundaries and functional properties; (ii) a reductionist layer modeling the behavior of individual CI components; and (iii) a service layer that describes the functional relationships between components and the infrastructure at different levels of granularity.

An ontology design pattern to model CI interdependencies was proposed by Ref. [4] as part of the TERMINUS ontology. Crisis management [5] and risk assessment [6, 7] are two possible applications of ontologies modeling critical infrastructures [8].

In Rosato et al. [9], the authors focus on modeling cyber dependencies of a set of infrastructures in an urban context. In particular, a dependency matrix [10] was used to reveal the potential vulnerability of a given node to the unavailability, corruption, or disclosure of data from an interdependent node regardless of the current state of the shared data infrastructure.

[1] https://websites.fraunhofer.de/CIPedia/index.php/Interdependency.

The work of Michel et al. [11] allowed us to define a dependency matrix generated based on the analysis of CI disruptions gathered from public media in the Netherlands from 2004 to 2010. In particular, a specific set of news sources containing impact keywords were acquired by Google News and further organized to save information including the affected CI sector and service, the initiating event (if any), and its dependency on another affected CI service.

In Franchina et al. [12], the authors present a methodology able to classify critical infrastructures starting from citizenship basic needs and foresee possible cascading effects.

In the MARIS methodology, we address all types of dependencies (logical, cyber, and physical) that are modeled by a specific system dependency layer and acquire open data of CIs and points of interest in order to create an urban dependency layer that can be valuable for further CI dependency analysis.

3. The MARIS methodology

3.1 Overview

Dependencies and interdependencies increase the vulnerability of infrastructures as they allow failures and perturbations to propagate from one system to another with the consequence that an infrastructure, which is not directly affected by some event that undermines its functioning, can be perturbed by the lack of functionality coming from another infrastructure which is turn hit by the event. Whereas from a conceptual side, the phenomenon is clear, on the practical side, dependencies and interdependencies are responsible for producing complex phenomena as, for instance, propagation time-scales can be quite different depending on the first perturbed infrastructure and on the infrastructure where perturbation will flow. For example, whereas perturbation on an electrical line may affect a very short time scale (seconds or less), an electrical perturbation to the traffic system or the water distribution network may take hours to produce sizeable effects. In that, if one would consider a" dependency matrix" where row and columns represent infrastructures and the i-j element their interaction, such a matrix is highly nonsymmetric (the ij element may be largely different from the ji one) as some infrastructure might perturb (severely and rapidly) other infrastructures which, in turn, have a very poor effect on the former when, in turn, perturbed. In some cases (i.e. when perturbation originates from the electrical system), the" coupling" strength is often very strong (i.e. many systems depend primarily on the electrical power), and the resulting reduction (or loss) of function established in a very short time scale. The presence of such strong coupling between infrastructures leads the system to be a" unique" system that cannot be treated and approximated as a system of independent (or nearly independent) infrastructure but as a" system of systems" that cannot be linearized A further element which leads the interdependency problem even more complex to be treated originates from the possibility of closed loops involving more than a couple of infrastructures. Perturbation from a first infrastructure might flow on several infrastructures before returning to the first one, providing negative feedback.

All these issues lead to an operational approach to interdependency that is extremely complex due primarily to an incomplete description of system's dependencies, time scales, and latencies. All dependency and interdependency data can be achieved through direct and indirect methods [12], but a complete theory of interdependency is still lacking.

Despite all that, it is possible to empirically deal with the problem of describing a number of dependent and interdependent systems with the aim of providing some type of decision support systems (DSS) enable to support decision makers (e.g., CI and Civil Protection managers) in the risk management process.

The MARIS methodology makes it possible to transform the layer of interdependencies known at the system level into a layer of interdependencies at the level of the physical components that lie in an urban context, as shown in **Figure 1**.

In the following, first, we give some definitions of the main concepts involved in the MARIS methodology, and then, we give an overview of its main steps.

3.2 Definitions

The MARIS methodology is based on seven fundamental concepts pertaining to the two above-mentioned layers. The ones dealing with the system dependency layer are the following:

- *System:* It denotes a Critical infrastructure from an overarching perspective [13]. Accordingly, examples are transportation, energy, water, waste, telecommunication, education, and health.

- *Subsystem:* It represents a further refinement of a system; for instance, the Water system includes several subsystems such as drinking water, wastewater/sewage, and stemming of surface water.

- *Subsystem Dependencies:* These can be physical, logical, and cyber. For example, a hospital depends on an electric distribution network.

Those pertaining to the urban infrastructure layer are:

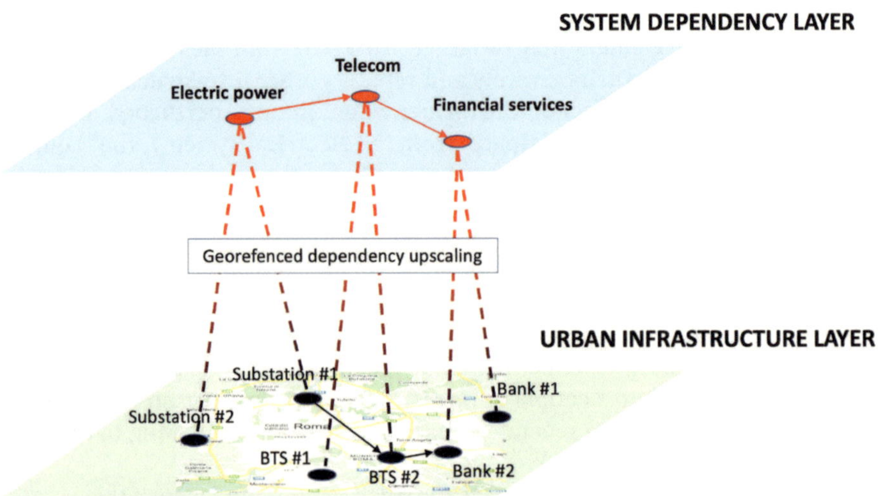

Figure 1.
Georeferenced dependency upscaling.

- *Entity Type:* It represents a physical component of a subsystem that is responsible for the provision of a service (e.g., the generic *substation* component of a distribution power grid).

- *Item:* It represents the resource, good, data, or functionality provided to a customer (or a citizen) that is produced and/or consumed by an entity.

- *Entity:* It represents the specific instance of an Entity Type (e.g., the set of substations of a distribution power grid in the area of interest).

- *Urban dependencies:* These can be physical, logical, and cyber. Unlike SD, UD involves Entity only. For example, a specific substation of a distribution power grid may depend on a nearby base transceiver station (BTS) that provides communication functionality required by the power grid's supervisory control and data acquisition (SCADA) system.

3.3 Main steps

Figure 2 describes the main steps of the MARIS methodology. First, dependencies at system scale are collected through a survey eliciting knowledge on the dependencies between critical infrastructures. As mentioned, these dependencies concern subsystems. Information on entities are retrieved from a GIS (Geographical Information System) such as OpenStreetMap (OSM). Then, similar to the approach presented in Ref. [14], subsystems are matched with entity types. The resulting pairs are included in an annotation table. Finally, all the above information, i.e., subsystems dependencies, entities, and the annotation table, are used to infer urban dependencies and create an interdependency graph.

4. Survey analysis on the dependencies between critical infrastructures

In this section, we present the results of a survey on Cis conducted with experts from Italy coming from various economic and social sectors.

This activity, in addition to providing a set of real interdependencies useful for the application of the MARIS methodology, was used as input to the DOMINO simulation model [12], developed by Tesseract Srl company, aiming at studying and quantifying the consequences of negative, unexpected, and disruptive events to the Supply and Value Chain systems of a country. The purpose of this model is to reproduce the impacts that would occur on such systems if relevant functions of the Chains were disrupted by natural or malicious events. This DOMINO approach leverages

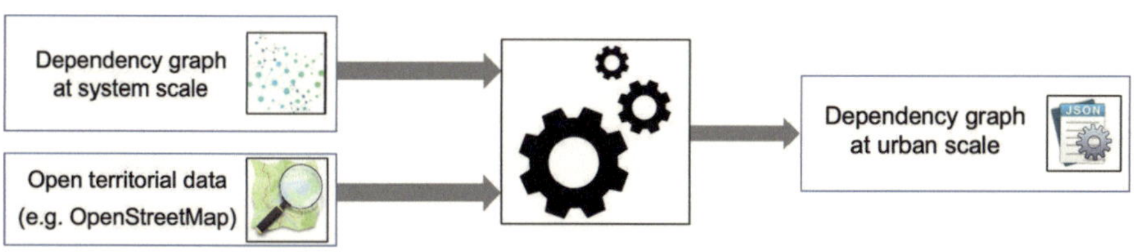

Figure 2.
Main steps of the MARIS methodology.

the concept of an *item* (as defined in Section 3.1) based on the NACE[2] and ATECO[3] classifications. The survey was conducted by involving industry experts to detail the direct consequences produced by their own organizations due to the loss (or degradation) of a specific item. In particular, for each of the 117 items considered (**Table A1** in the Appendix section), a set of the impacted items was collected. In addition, data regarding the duration of the propagation (in terms of hours, days, months, and years) were also collected in order to perform impact analysis through the DOMINO model.

The overall model will thus consider all the interdependencies between the various sectors (including Cis) that make up the Country Supply Chain System, based on the data reported by the various experts.

In the following, two examples of dependency trees are discussed. **Figures 3** and **4** show the direct dependencies of the *Drinking water* and *Bank* items respectively. At the top of each tree a timeline is displayed to show the "falling time" of each ITEM, starting from the "time zero," corresponding to the root node.

In the first dependency tree, it can be noted that, following the disruption of the *Drinking Water* item, two items, i.e., *Education* and *Research,* are impacted in the range of only 4 hours. On day 1, 45 items are impacted. Most of the dependencies represented are directly linked to the root node, but few of them are activated due to second (or higher) order effects (i.e., Maintenance services, Agriculture, and products).

In the second dependency tree, a few items are impacted in the order of a few minutes. However, most of the items are impacted after 3 days from the initiating failure.

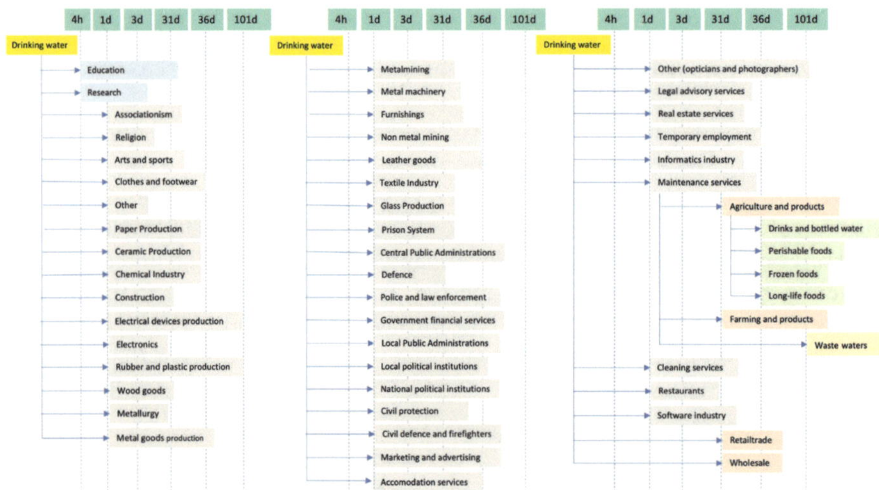

Figure 3.
DOMINO model from tesseract Srl: Drinking water dependency tree.

[2] https://www.en.wikipedia.org/wiki/Statistical_Classification_of_Economic_Activities_in_the_European_Community.

[3] https://www.istat.it/it/archivio/17888.

Figure 4.
DOMINO model from tesseract Srl: Bank dependency tree (items with impact higher than 30 days have been removed for the sake of space).

5. Case study

The case study concerns an area of the city of Rome characterized by a high concentration of various business activities and power centers, as well as the presence of CIs, which are essential to maintaining vital societal functions. As shown in **Table 1**, the mentioned area includes $N = 10$ systems and 11 subsystems.

5.1 System dependency layer

In this step, we imported the subset of subsystem dependencies that were collected by means of the survey described in Section 4. It is worth noting that these dependencies expand those more generic related to the system level, which are addressed, for instance, in Rinaldi et al. [2]. **Figure 5** shows an example of how system dependencies are extended to subsystem dependencies.

5.2 Territorial open-data acquisition

The development of the local dataset in the case study is based on the integration of open data collected and provided by OSM. The aim of this platform is to provide free geospatial information of world features. OSM uses open tagging mechanism to add meaning to geographic objects, so that any OSM user can add a new tag to them. For instance, some keys can be used to classify OSM entities into classes (e.g., highway, building, and amenity) while other keys play the role of attributes (e.g., name and maxspeed). OSM also allows to set attribute values, while values for classes are used to classify class members into categories (e.g., residential, hotel, monument).

System	Subsystem	Entity type	Entity occurrences
Education	University	Univ. building	27
	School	School building	181
	College	College building	11
Energy	Power	Substation facility	1000
Financial services	Bank	Bank building	413
	Insurance	Insurance building	40
Food	Restaurant	Restaurant building	2492
	Fast food	Fast food building	701
Government	Embassy	Embassy building	184
	Parliament	Parliament	2
Health	Clinic	Clinic building	40
	Pharmacy	Pharmacy building	506
	Hospital	Hospital facility	31
	Dentist	Dentist building	48
Internet	Internet services	Street cabinet	34
Telecommunication	Telecom	BTS building	122
Transportation	Railway	Railway Station	188
	Airports	Airport facility	4
Water	Water Supply	Water tower	2
Total:			6025

Table 1.
Dataset of infrastructure types in this study, categorized under 11 subsystems and 10 systems in the area of interest.

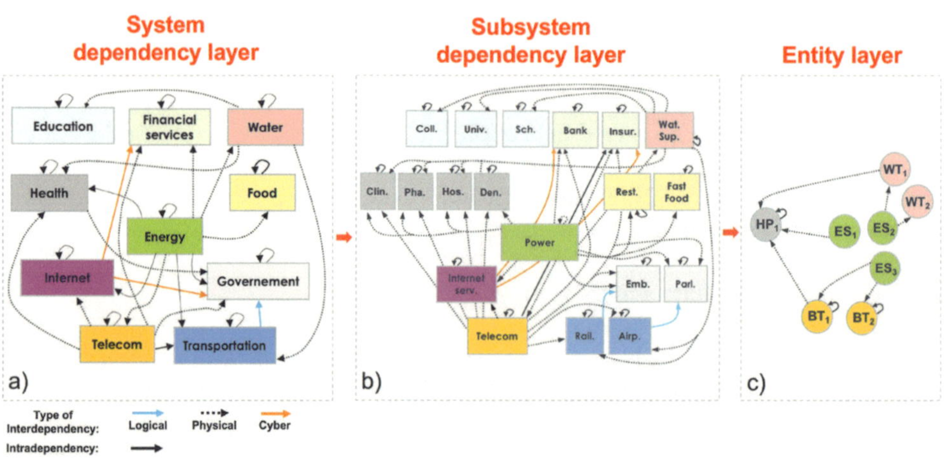

Figure 5.
(a) Example of system dependency layer; (b) example of subsystem dependency layer obtained from open data in the area of interest; (c) a fragment of the entity layer.

In order to facilitate the understanding of OSM data and reduce the number of incorrect entity-classes associations [15], we used the Taginfo platform[4] to gather tag statistics (e.g., providing the tags are actually in the database, the number of users choosing those tags) and to semantically enrich the entities. For example, when analyzing the railway subsystem, by setting the tag *railway = station* in Taginfo, we were able to select the railway station entities located in the area of interest and discard those combinations (e.g., railway = crossing, railway = radio) that were associated with different concepts.

Then, we used *Overpass turbo*[5], a web-based data mining tool for OSM, to acquire the OSM data of interest representing entity type occurrences of **Table A1** (e.g., university buildings and water towers) according to a geoJSON data format.

Therefore, the GIS open data acquired for CIs and Points of Interest were classified according to the specific subsystem.

5.3 Urban infrastructure layer

Regarding the dependencies to be associated to the entity layer, we considered those at the subsystem level and scaled them to the entity level. In other words, given that, according to the system dependency layer, the health system depends on the energy system, when scaling to the entity layer, we adopted the criterion that the specific hospital X depends on the energy supplied by the electrical substation Y (in particular, the one closest to the hospital).

Figure 5 shows the result of the application of the MARIS workflow, i.e., a fragment of the dependency at an urban level graph. It can be noticed that a geographical proximity criterion was applied to set up dependencies between CI components.

6. Conclusion

The presented MARIS methodology allows the generation of a graph at urban scale that can capture the known dependencies of CIs and Points of interest and model those dependencies that are unknown (because of partial, uncertain, or sensitive data) through the application of proximity criteria.

The use of open software and data (Taginfo, Overpass turbo, OSM) and the knowledge of CI interdependencies data at the system level were used to estimate the interdependencies at an urban level and to produce a realistic graph of interdependencies.

The methodology was applied to the city of Rome to create an interdependency graph characterized by 6025 entities representing real CIs and Points of interest. Future developments will concern the application of dynamic simulation models to the interdependency graph, obtained through the MARIS methodology, in order to reproduce the impacts that would occur on such systems when relevant functions of the supply chain of an area of interest were disrupted by natural or anthropic events.

---

[4] http://taginfo.openstreetmap.org.

[5] Overpass-turbo.eu.

Appendix A

List of items considered in the DOMINO model

System	Item
Water	Irrigation Water
Water	Water For Industrial Use
Water	Water For Industrial Use
Agriculture, Livestock, Fisheries, Forests	Agriculture And Products
Agriculture, Livestock, Fisheries, Forests	Farming And Products
Agriculture, Livestock, Fisheries, Forests	Forests
Agriculture, Livestock, Fisheries, Forests	Lumber
Agriculture, Livestock, Fisheries, Forests	Fisheries And Products
Environment	Waste Water
Environment	Dams
Environment	Nonhazardous Waste
Environment	Hazardous Waste
Environment	Meteorology and Climate Services
Food Chain	Long-Life Foods
Food Chain	Perishable Foods
Food Chain	Frozen Foods
Food Chain	Drinks and Bottled Water
Trade	Retail Trade
Trade	Wholesale
Culture, Icons, Venues	Arts and Sports
Culture, Icons, Venues	Associationism
Culture, Icons, Venues	Education
Culture, Icons, Venues	Religion
Culture, Icons, Venues	Research
Energy	Coal
Energy	Fuels (Oil, Diesel, Biodiesel, etc.)
Energy	Electricity distribution
Energy	Renewable Sources Biomass
Energy	Wind Renewable Sources
Energy	Geothermal Renewable Sources
Energy	Renewable Water Sources
Energy	Solar Renewable Sources
Energy	Liquid Natural Gas
Energy	Greggio
Energy	Methane
Energy	Nuclear
Energy	Electric Transport
Energy	Electricity Production

System	Item
Finance	Insurance, Reinsurance, and Pension Funds
Finance	Cash
Finance	Stock Market
Finance	Loans And Mortgages
Finance	Banks
Finance	Services and Payment Systems (Excluding Cash)
Industry	Clothes and Footwear
Industry	Other
Industry	Paper Production
Industry	Chemical Industry
Industry	Construction
Industry	Electrical Devices Production
Industry	Electronics
Industry	Rubber and Plastics Production
Industry	Metal Machinery
Industry	Metallurgy
Industry	Nonmetal Mining
Industry	Metal Mining
Industry	Furniture and Supply Chain
Industry	Leather Goods
Industry	Ceramic Production
Industry	Wood Goods
Industry	Metal Goods Production
Industry	Textile Industry
Industry	Glass and the Supply Chain
Institutions and Public Administration	Central Public Administrations
Institutions and Public Administration	Local Public Administrations
Institutions and Public Administration	Civil Defense and Firefighters
Institutions and Public Administration	Police and Law Enforcement
Institutions and public administration	Local political institutions
Institutions and Public Administration	National Political Institutions
Institutions and Public Administration	Civil Protection
Institutions and Public Administration	Government Financial Services
Institutions and Public Administration	Prison System
Institutions and Public Administration	Defense
Manpower	Physical Manpower
Manpower	Virtual Manpower
Healthcare	Social Assistance
Healthcare	Production of Medicines and Medical Devices
Healthcare	Health Emergency Services
Healthcare	Private Medical Services

System	Item
Healthcare	Public Medical Services
Healthcare	Veterinary Services
Healthcare	Sale of Medicines and Medical Devices
Services	Other (Opticians and Photographers)
Services	Legal Estate Services
Services	Legal Advisory Services
Services	Informatics Industry
Services	Temporary Employment
Services	Marketing and Advertising
Services	Restaurants
Services	Accommodation Services
Services	Maintenance Services
Services	Cleaning Services
Services	Private Security Services
Services	Software Industry
ICT	Digital Terrestrial Connection System
ICT	Data Processing, Hosting
ICT	Provision of Internet Services (Isp)
ICT	Web Portals
ICT	Television Production
ICT	Publishing (Books, Periodicals, and Newspapers)
ICT	Radio Broadcasting
ICT	Radio and Communication Services
ICT	Satellite Services
ICT	Fixed Telecommunications
ICT	Fiber Optic Telecommunications
ICT	Mobile Telecommunications
Transport and Logistics	Air Transport of Goods and Logistics
Transport and Logistics	Passenger Air Transport
Transport and logistics	Logistics by sea and ocean
Transport And Logistics	Logistics By Road
Transport And Logistics	Transport On Inland Waterways
Transport And Logistics	Rail Freight And Logistics Transport
Transport And Logistics	Passenger Rail Transport

Table A1.
List of items.

Author details

Antonio Di Pietro[1*], Alessandro Calabrese[2], Antonio De Nicola[1], Daniele Ferneti[3], Luisa Franchina[2], Josè Martì[4] and Tommaso Ruocco[2]

1 ENEA, Casaccia Research Centre, Rome, Italy

2 Tesseract srl, Rome, Italy

3 Sapienza University of Rome, Roma, RM, Italy

4 Department of Electrical and Computer Engineering, University of British Columbia, Vancouver, B.C., Canada

*Address all correspondence to: antonio.dipietro@enea.it

IntechOpen

© 2023 The Author(s). Licensee IntechOpen. This chapter is distributed under the terms of the Creative Commons Attribution License (http://creativecommons.org/licenses/by/3.0), which permits unrestricted use, distribution, and reproduction in any medium, provided the original work is properly cited.

References

[1] Laugé A, Hernantes J, Sarriegi JM. Critical infrastructure dependencies: A holistic, dynamic and quantitative approach. International Journal of Critical Infrastructure Protection. 2015;**8**:16-23. DOI: 10.1016/j.ijcip.2014.12.004. Available from: https://www.sciencedirect.com/science/article/pii/S187454821400081X

[2] Rinaldi SM, Peerenboom JP, Kelly TK. Identifying, understanding, and analyzing critical infrastructure interdependencies. IEEE Control Systems Magazine. 2001;**21**(6):11-25. DOI: 10.1109/37.969131

[3] Foglietta C, Panzieri S, Pascucci F. Algorithms and tools for risk/impact evaluation in critical infrastructures. International Journal of Critical Infrastructures. 2015;**565**:227-238. DOI: 10.1007/978-3-662-44160-2_8

[4] Coletti A, De Nicola A, Vicoli G, Villani ML. Semantic modeling of cascading risks in interoperable socio-technical systems. In: Popplewell K, Thoben K-D, Knothe T, Poler R, editors. Enterprise Interoperability viii. Cham: Springer International Publishing; 2019. pp. 119-129

[5] Nicola D, Antonio MM, Villani ML. Creative design of emergency management scenarios driven by semantics: An application to smart cities. Information Systems. 2019;**81**:21-48. DOI: 10.1016/j.is.2018.10.005. Available from: https://www.sciencedirect.com/science/article/pii/S0306437918304277

[6] Coletti A, De Nicola A, Villani ML. Building climate change into risk assessments. Natural Hazards. 2016;**84**(2):1307-1325. DOI: 10.1007/s11069-016-2487-6

[7] Coletti A, De Nicola A, Di Pietro A, La Porta L, Pollino M, Rosato V, et al. A comprehensive system for semantic spatiotemporal assessment of risk in urban areas. Journal of Contingencies and Crisis Management. 2020;**28**(3):178-193. DOI: 10.1111/1468-5973.12309. Available from: https://onlinelibrary.wiley.com

[8] Antonio DN, Villani ML. Smart city ontologies and their applications: A systematic literature review. Sustainability. 2021;**13**(10):20-60. DOI: 10.3390/su13105578. Available from: https://www.mdpi.com/2071-1050/13/10/5578

[9] Rosato V, Di Pietro A, Kotzanikolaou P, Stergiopoulos G, Smedile G. Integrating resilience in time-based dependency analysis: A large-scale case study for urban critical infrastructures. In: Rosato V, Di Pietro A, editors. Issues on Risk Analysis for Critical Infrastructure Protection, Chap. 5. Rijeka: IntechOpen; 2021. DOI: 10.5772/intechopen.97809

[10] Macaulay T. Critical Infrastructure: Understanding its Component Parts, Vulnerabilities, Operating Risks, and Interdependencies. Taylor & Francis; 2008

[11] Eeten M, Nieuwenhuijs A, Luiijf E, Klaver M, Cruz E. The state and the threat of cascading failure across critical infrastructures: The implications of empirical evidence from media incident reports. Public Administration. 2011;**89**:381. DOI: 10.1111/j.1467-9299.2011.01926.x

[12] Franchina L, Carbonelli M, Crisci M, Gratta L, Perucchini D. An effective approach for cascading effects prevision in critical infrastructures. Studies in Computational Intelligence. 2011a;**7**: 73-90. DOI: 10.1504/IJCIS.2011.038958

[13] Nirandjan S, Koks EE, Ward PJ, Aerts JCJH. A spatially-explicit harmonized global dataset of critical infrastructure. Scientific Data. 2022;**9**(1):150. DOI: 10.1038/s41597-022-01218-4

[14] Minardi R, Villani ML, De Nicola A. Semantic reasoning for geolocalized assessment of crime risk in smart cities. Smart Cities. 2023;**6**(1):179-195. DOI: 10.3390/smartcities6010010. Available from: https://www.mdpi.com/2624-6511/6/1/10

[15] Ali AL, Schmid F. Data quality assurance for volunteered geographic information. In: Duckham M, Pebesma E, Stewart K, Frank AU, editors. Geographic Information Science. Cham: Springer International Publishing; 2014. pp. 126-141

Chapter 4

Science Gateways and AI/ML: How Can Gateway Concepts and Solutions Meet the Needs in Data Science?

Sandra Gesing, Marlon Pierce, Suresh Marru, Michael Zentner, Kathryn Huff, Shannon Bradley, Sean B. Cleveland, Steven R. Brandt, Rajiv Ramnath, Kerk Kee, Maytal Dahan, Braulio M. Villegas Martínez, Wilmer Contreras Sepulveda and José J. Sánchez Mondragón

Abstract

Science gateways are a crucial component of critical infrastructure as they provide the means for users to focus on their topics and methods instead of the technical details of the infrastructure. They are defined as end-to-end solutions for accessing data, software, computing services, sensors, and equipment specific to the needs of a science or engineering discipline and their goal is to hide the complexity of the underlying infrastructure. Science gateways are often called Virtual Research Environments in Europe and Virtual Labs in Australasia; we consider these two terms to be synonymous with science gateways. Over the past decade, artificial intelligence (AI) and machine learning (ML) have found applications in many different fields in private industry, and private industry has reaped the benefits. Likewise, in the academic realm, large-scale data science applications have also learned to apply public high-performance computing resources to make use of this technology. However, academic and research science gateways have yet to fully adopt the tools of AI. There is an opportunity in the gateways space, both to increase the visibility and accessibility to AI/ML applications and to enable researchers and developers to advance the field of science gateway cyberinfrastructure itself. Harnessing AI/ML is recognized as a high priority by the science gateway community. It is, therefore, critical for the next generation of science gateways to adapt to support the AI/ML that is already transforming many scientific fields. The goal is to increase collaborations between the two fields and to ensure that gateway services are used and are valuable to the AI/ML community. This chapter presents state-of-the-art examples and areas of opportunity for the science gateways community to pursue in relation to AI/ML and some vision of where these new capabilities might impact science gateways and support scientific research.

IntechOpen

Keywords: science gateways, virtual research environments, artificial intelligence, machine learning, collaboration

1. Introduction

Science gateways are end-to-end solutions for accessing data, software, computing services, and equipment specific to the needs of a science or engineering discipline. The goal of science gateways is to hide the complexity of the underlying research infrastructure and to enable scientists and educators to focus on their research and teaching—science gateways form one of the building blocks for critical infrastructure in research. Science gateways are often called Virtual Research Environments (VREs) in Europe and Virtual Labs (VLs) in Australasia [1]; we consider these two terms to be synonymous with science gateways. While quite a few research domains such as the life sciences, chemistry, and geospatial sciences have adapted the use of science gateways, there is still the need for a larger uptake in those domains and for broadening participation to further domains and user groups such as high-school students [2].

Some artificial intelligence/machine learning (AI/ML) research is supported by science gateways. Usually, this in the form of "software-as-a-service" for developed and trained AI/ML applications, for example, AI4Mars [3] on Zooniverse [4] that offers science gateways as a service for citizen sciences (see **Figure 1**).

Even though AI/ML and science gateways are both well-anchored in the high-performance computing (HPC) community, the field of science gateways still has low visibility to AI/ML application developers and users. A reason for the small degree of overlap of the AI community with the science gateway community includes that the AI/ML community has focused more on developer tools and languages than on intuitive and graphical interfaces. The trajectory of new concepts in academia is often first to develop effective methods, second to increase their efficiency and then, finally, to open them up to a wider community via considering usability. In the case of AI/ML it means to enhance the visibility via a set of capabilities that support AI/ML development and improve the uptake of science gateways in the AI/ML community. Furthermore, there is a need to advance the field of science gateway cyberinfrastructure itself.

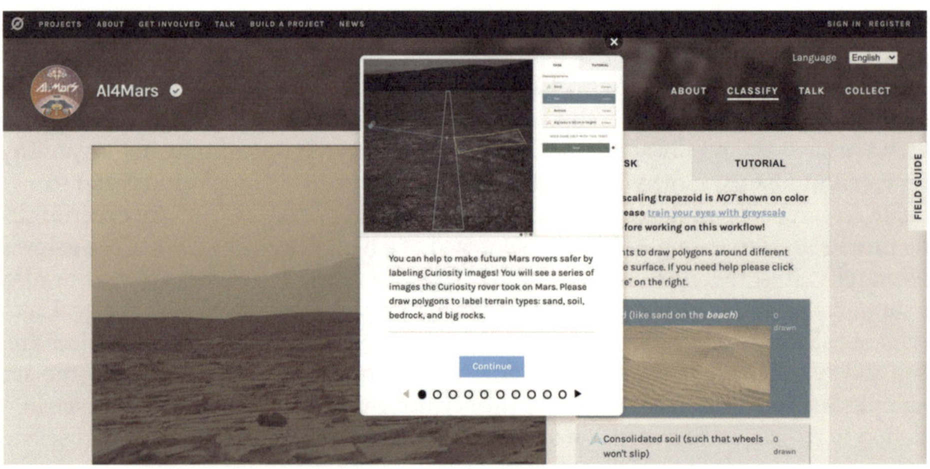

Figure 1.
The project AI4Mars uses citizen sciences to teach Mars rovers how to classify martian terrain.

These topics are critical for the next generation of science gateways and its community as AI/ML is already transforming many scientific fields.

One goal of science gateways is to facilitate collaborations between highly technical practitioners and less computer-savvy researchers, and thereby expand the reach and impact of science. In this case, it means to make AI/ML services accessible to the community. This chapter is part of the work to investigate the target groups in AI/ML research and to identify the opportunities and activities needed to achieve this goal and contribute significantly to critical infrastructure in research, teaching, and beyond.

For promoting collaborations between the science gateway community and the AI/ML community, it is important to target the three major groups: academic communities, funding agencies, and industry. Important actors in the science gateway community for increasing the collaboration are providers and developers of mature science gateway frameworks such as HUBzero [5], Apache Airavata [6], and Tapis [7]. Thus, in the area of academic communities, they can organize special tracks at Gateways conferences [8], which allow more conversations and exchanges of ideas in various science gateway communities including users of science gateways. Another possibility for widening the outreach is to hold webinars, panels, birds-of-a-feather sessions, and similar outreach efforts at conferences such as Practice & Experience in Advanced Research Computing (PEARC) [9], eScience [10], and Supercomputing [11] to promote the use of science gateways to research computing and interdisciplinary research communities, including AI/ML experts attracted by these conferences.

Another way to reach AI researchers is at their domain-specific conferences. Presentations at appropriate AI conferences would raise awareness of the concept of science gateways and would elucidate the opportunities to address pain points regarding usability and integration with complex computing and data infrastructures, for example, the International Conference on Machine Learning, Optimization and Data Science [12]. Papers could be "crowd-sourced" as previous papers to International Workshop on Science Gateways (IWSG) [13] or this manuscript.

Funding agencies and funded institutes/large projects around AI form another important target group for gathering requirements on usability and accessibility of AI/ML methods.

Examples of outreach to these groups include the promotion of science gateways to AI/ML award winners, especially at the various AI institutes [14] funded by National Science Foundation (NSF), and contacting cognizant program officers of AI/ML research-supporting programs to discuss roles for science gateways. While science gateways are well known in NSF directorates such as Office of Advanced Cyberinfrastructure (OAC) [15], program officers in other NSF directorates or other federal agencies might be less familiar with or not yet know about science gateways. In the 2019 update to the NSF National Artificial Intelligence Research and Development Strategic Plan [16], one of the major topics was the recognition of the gap between the capabilities of AI algorithms and the usability of AI systems by humans. The report states "Human-aware intelligent systems are needed that can interact intuitively with users and enable seamless machine–human collaborations." This is exactly the goal of science gateways and the fact that they are not mentioned as a potential solution emphasizes the point that science gateways are not yet well known in the AI community.

As a large producer and user of AI/ML concepts and technologies, industry is an important target group, especially projects that foster collaboration of funding agencies and companies, that is, a collaboration between Amazon and NSF that funds ten

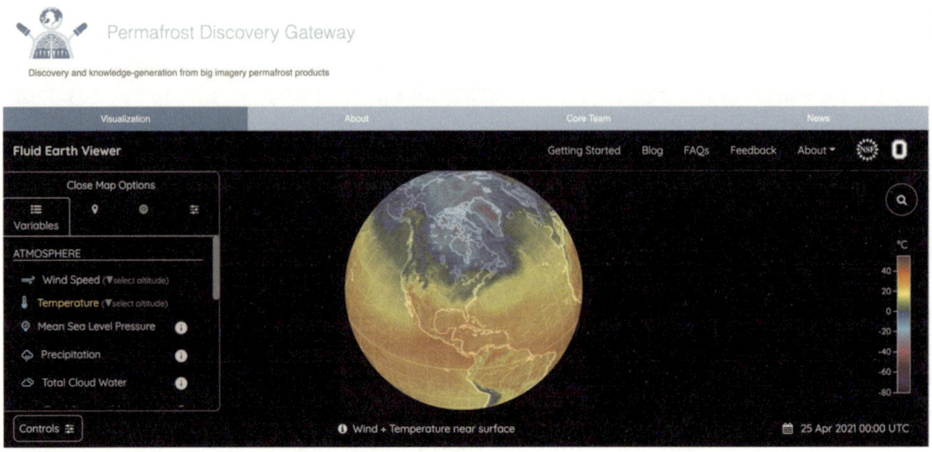

Figure 2.
The Permafrost Discovery Gateway uses AI to provide access to pan-Arctic permafrost knowledge and information about the globe regarding pan-Arctic change.

research projects on fairness of AI [17]. The uptake of science gateways in industry is one of the goals some science gateway providers pursue for widening their community. Such adoption is also a measure of the sustainability achieved by science gateway frameworks. Meaningful connections include to introduce science gateways to technology providers, especially those in the space of cloud services such as Omnibond Systems who are already part of the science gateways community.

While there is interest especially from science gateway providers to form collaborations with academic communities, industry, and funding agencies, it is important to carefully select content to be presented to the target audiences. In order to achieve a wide outreach, we aim at answering an overarching question: how can Gateway concepts and solutions meet the needs of data science? In order to answer this question, the chapter is laid out with the following sections: first, we provide a brief background on AI, ML, and data-intensive computing in general. Second, we explain the terminologies, especially the difference between AI, ML, and data-intensive computing. Third, we explain what science gateways can do and describe their general capabilities. In this section, we also provide example gateways across different disciplines. Fourth, we discuss several science gateway opportunities for AI/ML research. Finally, we wrap up the chapter with the future outlook (**Figure 2**).

2. Background

Since its introduction [18], interest in AI has gone through several peaks and troughs. Generally, peaks have been driven by algorithmic progress coupled with the availability of appropriate computing resources and the troughs by their lack. This in particular has been true of brute force algorithms and shortcut modifications to those algorithms that prune brute force exploration. Contemporary with the notion of AI was the publication of the foundations of neural networks [19]. Although first appearing at a similar point in time, neural networks only began receiving widespread attention as a means for ML when software libraries and products became available to allow nonexperts to test the application of neural networks within their own research domains, especially during the 1980s. After a great wave of progress, limitations of existing neural network topologies and training algorithms were realized, spawning decades of research into more effective ways to represent and compute upon neural networks.

One of the confounding factors for early progress on ML was the need for ML algorithms to be fed by large amounts of training data. In many domains, such training sets did not exist. However, one of the significant drivers of progress in this area has been the emergence of the Internet. The past three decades has seen the creation of massive training sets in the form of user actions on the Internet, immense corpi of content authored by people participating in the Internet, large libraries of images and video becoming widely available, and so forth. Another key force in creating training sets has been the advancement of massively parallel supercomputer resources (e.g., XSEDE [20], OSG [21]) that can compute large amounts of data using physics-based models, which subsequently can be used to produce ML-based approximate models to rapidly compute these same outputs. These decades have also created a paired interest in ML involving both scientific and commercial interests. Although this pairing creates a variety of potential ethical issues, it has driven progress in this field at a rate faster than most fields that lack this symbiosis. It has even seen commercial organizations making ML algorithms available to the public (e.g., see Abadi et al. [22]).

Based on this history, today AI, ML, and (more generally) data-intensive computing have been identified as high priorities for federally funded research. In both 2016 [23] and 2019 [16, 24], reports by the National Science & Technology Council, spanning two different presidential administrations. In response, comprehensive programs and funding priorities have been put forward by federal agencies including the NSF [25], DARPA [26], NIH [27], and DOE [28]. AI/ML methods are also high priorities for mission-driven science agencies such as National Aeronautics and Space Administration (NASA). National Institute and Standards and Technology (NIST) is leading efforts related to safety and benchmarking of AI/ML applications. Many government agencies are releasing large, curated data sets that can be used for training.

The applications of AI/ML research are scientifically promising, of strategic importance to national defense, and important for economic competitiveness. Research utilizing AI/ML is expanding in multiple specific domains, including big data and high-energy physics, astronomy, animal husbandry, agriculture (Ag), food security, climate change, and city infrastructure. The AI100 Project [29] and the Computing Community Consortium [30], as well as the National Science & Technology Council Reports, provide long-range overviews of AI/ML research challenges and opportunities, including their likely impacts on society as a whole.

Science gateways are widely known to bring advanced scientific capabilities to researchers in the form of data sets, HPC resources, and instruments such that researchers do not need to be experts in accessing those resources [31]. Today, we face another evolution in AI/ML, where it can be further democratized and advanced through the use of science gateways. This overview examines the opportunities for integrating AI/ML research with science gateway cyberinfrastructure, based on the extensive background information surveyed above.

3. Terminology

Following Stone et al. [30], we will distinguish AI, ML, and data-intensive computing as follows:

- AI is a branch of computer science that studies intelligence by synthesizing intelligence. AI is a broad field that encompasses subfields that include ML, autonomous systems, simulations of biologically based intelligence, and other fields.
- ML is a branch of AI that examines algorithms and methods by which computer programs can be taught to recognize patterns in data sets for purposes such as classification, recognition (i.e., facial, speech, and character), recommendation, surrogate models, and decision-making, among others.
- Data-intensive computing is a general term for computing that consumes large amounts of data, either streaming or static, as input, presenting challenging problems for scalably integrating storage, computing, and I/O. ML methods may be used in data-intensive computing.

This overview focuses on the requirements of ML methods that are being applied to a wide range of scientific data in diverse scientific fields in support of scientific research. ML holds the promise for scalably extracting information and knowledge (including scientific insights) from the large amounts of data generated by both experiments at all scales as well as scientific simulations, and fits well with the capabilities of science gateways today.

4. Science gateway infrastructure

Science gateways in general are noted for their ability to provide the following capabilities to support scientific research:

- Simplified access to research computing and storage resources.
- Ability to provide scientific software as a service.
- Ability to integrate diverse, distributed computing and data into a single platform.
- Ability to provide a range of scientific and engineering environments that support diverse stakeholder groups in a particular community.
- Ability to securely control access to resources and data.
- Support scientific collaboration through the sharing of access to results.
- Support for reproducibility of computational results.

In other words, we can consider science gateways as cyberinfrastructure environments to support Findable, Accessible, Interoperable, and Reusable (FAIR) research [32]. Many of the concerns and opportunities identified in [16, 23, 24] for the use of AI/ML research are FAIR challenges. The FAIR principles have created significant momentum in the research community recognizing a need to improve the quality of research by establishing common standards. However, bridging the principles with the research infrastructure remains a challenging task due to its diversity and domain-specific nature of tasks. Science gateways provide an excellent opportunity to achieve FAIRness of research data and software.

4.1 Use cases in artificial intelligence

4.1.1 Physics

International collaboration is often basic for our scientific development, and these efforts are at the core of its infrastructure. Researchers are partnering with NSF and DOE to study how AI Frameworks can be leveraged in physics research. One such project, ML and FPGA Computing for Real-Time Application in Big-Data Physics Experiments as a science driver investigates the creation of a FAIR framework for AI [33]. Example is a project focusing on Inspired Artificial Intelligence in High-Energy Physics which builds on the successes of the last years with the Large Hadron Collider (LHC) and the combination of the Laser Interferometer Gravitational—wave Observatory (LIGO) and the Large Synoptic Survey Telescope (LSST) for Multi-Messenger Astrophysics by making artificial AI models and data more accessible and reusable with the goal to accelerate research and outperform current approaches [34]. Broad international collaborations as the Event Horizon Telescope (EHT) are excellent opportunities to introduce science gateways. This single-event global array of eight ground-based radio telescopes aimed at obtaining the image a black hole and its shadow could become a n international mainstay [35].

4.1.2 Photonics and quantum optics

AI is already taking part in the development of future technologies, as is the case of the quantum technologies. In this case, the integration of two communities, AI and photonics, have become complementary during the last decades, where ML protocols are being matched to photonic platforms giving rise to photonic neural network architecture [36]. The applications of AI, especially neural networks and ML in the field of quantum optics have also become prevalent for experimental setups used for classification and identification of light sources and quantum states by using these two approaches [37–39]. Such examples with computational properties have low-complexity and low-cost implementations promising quantum architecture that could apply underlying cyberinfrastructure enabling users to create their own workflows to run simulations codes. Those applications designed by the quantum community would generate tools with unprecedented capabilities available to researchers unfamiliar with the world of quantum optics and photonics.

4.1.3 Astronomy

The goal of the AGNet [40] project is to leverage AI to develop a novel interdisciplinary approach combining astronomy big data with ML tools to build a deep learning algorithm to estimate the masses of super-massive black holes. Measuring the masses *via* traditional methods is very expensive and such a new algorithm could transform the field of cosmology.

4.1.4 Agriculture

The connection between AI and Ag seems obvious. One applies big-data analytics, ML, and deep learning algorithms in geospatial information systems (GIS), satellite data, lidar information, sensor data, and other tools and technologies to improve crops [41]. However, the connection is not as clear when discussing animal husbandry. An AI tool Project [42], Solving Dairy Cattle Genetic Improvement Challenges using Deep Learning, will use AI "to identify cattle that have the highest genetic potential for milk production and health status and make simplistic assumptions about the relationship between phenotypes and genotypes." Another interesting connection between AI and Ag is in the area of Food Security [43]. The Alan Turing Institute [18] is using ML and AI to leverage data and models of plant development, plant pathology, crop yields, and climate science to form a cohesive national crop modeling framework for the United Kingdom.

4.1.5 Climate change

The impact of climate change on the planet is much discussed in the news, but the ability to understand the true influence is limited by the ability to quantify how multiple factors work together to impact this change. The Permafrost Discovery Gateway [44] is using AI to assist with the management of ingesting large amounts of remote sensing data into machine and deep learning models which will ultimately provide "access to pan-Arctic permafrost knowledge, which can immediately inform the economy, security, and resilience of the Nation, the Arctic region, and the globe with respect to pan-Arctic change."

4.1.6 Urban planning

What do roads, sidewalks, parks, access to food and medical care, and even tree canopies providing shade on roads and sidewalks have to do with AI? Many studies have been done on food deserts and transit deserts, but by leveraging AI, researchers are able to look at all different types of neighborhood-scale infrastructure [45] (see **Figure 3**). By identifying infrastructure deserts, communities' ability to deal with them will be strengthened in the long term, particularly in low-income communities.

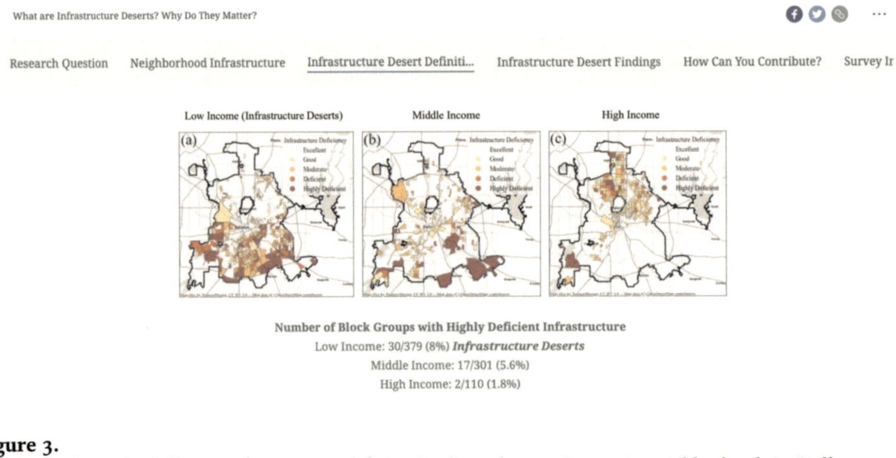

Figure 3.
The figure shows the different infrastructure deficiencies dependent on income in neighborhoods in Dallas.

4.1.7 Biology

Concerned with the detection of Regulatory Elements using GRO-seq data, the dREG science gateway [46] identifies the location of DNA sequence regions known as transcript regulation elements including promoters and enhancers—the critical components of the genetic regulatory programs of all organisms. The dREG computational code itself uses a support vector machines-based model trained by large-scale data. This science gateway democratizes the use of these sophisticated ML techniques to a wider community. The gateway interfaces with XSEDE compute infrastructures for seamlessly enabling access to compute intensive training and prediction phases. On the front-end of these ML models, user-friendly data visualization interfaces enable a wider community to interact with bigWig data, dREG signal predictions, and genome coordinates of peaks of transcriptions.

4.1.8 Humanities

Snow Vision uses image classification methods to identify pottery sherds created by Native Americans of the US Southeast. The Snow Vision science gateway [47] enables the humanities community to utilize ML-based matching algorithms to compare user uploaded sherd images to identify the original stamped designs from which their fragments descend. The gateway makes available the matching algorithms implemented by a deep-learning Point Cloud Library (PCL) for generating depth maps from 3D sherd image files and Caffe [48] deep learning toolkit.

5. Science gateways, quantum computing, and artificial intelligence

New paradigms in computing open up novel areas for exploring the potential of science gateways and AI/ML. A future direction is the emerging paradigm of quantum computing which uses the fundamental properties of quantum mechanics, such as superposition, entanglement, and interference. This domain strongly differs from classical computing, where one data qubit is equivalent to two classical bits of information. This feature is a promising solution for higher computational power within shorter calculation time, which is very useful for artificial neural networks and ML. At this stage, the latest frontier of computation relies on the hybrid development of these two areas in quantum computing and how both could support each other in the evolution of classification and clustering of big classical-to-quantum data. While the topic of AI and ML is well established in computer sciences, both are quite novel approaches on the science and technology side and not fully adapted yet. We analyzed where ML has developed better among those different fields and where it has moved to Quantum computation, more specifically, in the Quantum Machine Learning (QML) frontier. We have used Scopus data to show (after a normalization) in which of the sciences have become more active. A Scopus search on ML will provide us with the following fields list:

1. Computer Science

2. Engineering

3. Mathematics
4. Medicine
5. Physics and Astronomy
6. Biochemistry, Genetics and Molecular Biology
7. Decision Sciences
8. Materials Science
9. Social Sciences
10. Energy
11. Earth and Planetary Sciences
12. Environmental Science
13. Chemistry
14. Neuroscience
15. Business, Management and Accounting
16. Agricultural and Biological Sciences
17. Chemical Engineering
18. Multidisciplinary
19. Arts and Humanities
20. Health Professions
21. Pharmacology, Toxicology and Pharmaceutics
22. Immunology and Microbiolog
23. Psychology
24. Economics, Econometrics and Finance

Figure 4 provides those answers by displaying in blue the above fields list and in orange those in QML. The striking disparity on Physics and Astronomy (5), Materials Science (8) and Chemistry (13) can be explained from their expected larger processing demands. Besides, the actual growth of QML has happened in a much shorter timespan but pursues the very active growth shown in ML. Therefore, larger uptake of ML and QML is a fundamental need and can be improved by introducing science gateways.

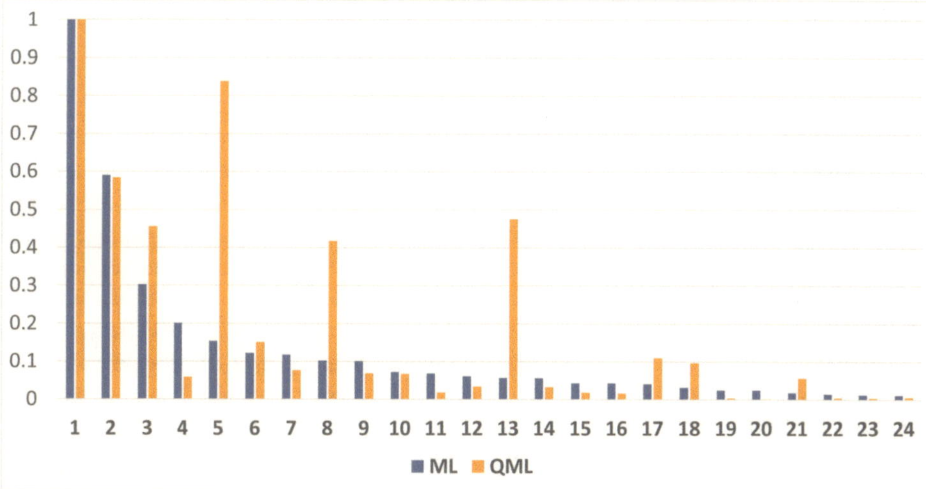

Figure 4.
Distributions of QML (orange bar chart) and ML (blue bar chart) into the different fields of Science and Technology. The uptake of QML on ML is described by normalization ratio of QML/ML of 139.6.

6. The theoretical framework for science gateways in AI/ML research

AI/ML research faces following challenges that can be addressed by a theoretical framework for integration with science gateways. Each challenge is part of the research question how science gateways can improve AI/ML research and add aspects that are not well considered as part of the AI/ML research yet.

6.1 Availability

Providing software-as-a-service is a common mode of operation for science gateways. Many gateways are already providing trained ML methods to their user communities. In this sense, an ML application is just another piece of software that a gateway can provide, simplifying access and helping to ensure the software is up to date, is used in the correct way, and is installed on adequate resources.

High-performance AI/ML is a strategic priority, as it will be necessary for these methods to scale to support enormous data sets. Providing simplified access to HPC and other specialized resources is a strength of science gateways, particularly as the landscape of those resources evolves into Graphics Processing Unit (GPU), Field Programmable Gate Arrays (FPGA), and other environments tailored for efficient AI/ML. Various federal initiatives are promoting improved AI standards, access to benchmarked, open-source applications, and access to public data sets usable for training. Science gateways will provide access to these tools and data.

In science gateways, we typically consider AI/ML-based applications as having a target audience beyond that of the developer; that is, a developer has created an application and wants it to reach a larger user community. There is also an important scenario in which a researcher develops an AI/ML application to further their own research; the application itself may have no (or at least no perceived) broader use by others, at least in the initial phase. It is still essential that science gateways are available to support such research. Even if the software itself is never used again beyond the original scope, its results may be published and thus must be auditable and reproducible by reviewers and future readers.

6.2 Validity, reproducibility, transparency

Software based on ML methods is very different from traditional scientific software in that the ML-based applications must be trained on data sets. Thus, one must separately validate any results obtained from an ML-based application. Changes in training data sets will give different results, so it is important to track not only the versions of a particular software used but also the version of the trained model and the data sets used in training, including any processes for cleaning or otherwise filtering the data.

Gateways, in their role as supporting scientific software-as-a-service, are already well-positioned to at least support the collection of version metadata needed to support reproducibility or at least the provenance of how a particular result was achieved.

More broadly, many ML applications should be understood as dataflow programs that combine well-known algorithms into specific applications. Experiments to improve the workflow and the validation of the AI methods are currently performed outside most gateways and are considered publication quality research in such journals as *Nature Methods*. Capturing these processes is an important enhancement that could easily be supported by science gateways.

Minimally, a provider of an ML-based application could at least publish the metadata about how a particular application was developed, trained, and validated, but gateways themselves can also support these processes directly. This would enable users to reproduce and inspect the application itself and the training data. Gateways could furthermore track the development of alternative pipelines and trainings by both the code authors and the interested members of the community. This would provide direct support and supplemental information to the methods publications by the original authors.

6.3 Privacy

Data privacy is the obverse aspect of trustworthiness, since many ML applications may work with sensitive data such as personal health information and proprietary data. Science gateways can be used to support privacy for data sets by limiting access to data through controlled and auditable user and programming interfaces. These gateways can operate within privacy protected environments that support The Health Insurance Portability and Accountability Act (HIPAA), Federal Information Security Modernization Act (FISMA), and other regulated data classifications. Further limitations, such as differential privacy, are open-research areas that can also be supported by gateways.

6.4 Trustworthiness, explainability, and uncertainty quantification

Trustworthiness, explainability, and uncertainty quantification are larger open problems in AI/ML research. Trustworthiness of scientific results obtained from AI/ML methods in scientific applications can be increased through the ability of science gateways to support reproducibility, auditability, and transparency in tracking how a particular application was developed, trained, and validated. Gateways can serve as a focal point where experimental results, computational results, and AI/ML-based models can be cross compared and validated. Explainability is an open-research area, as the results of many current methods (most notably artificial neural networks) cannot be understood by humans, even if we have full access to the software and training data. However, as new, more explainable methods are developed, science gateways should be an important delivery mechanism. Science gateways may also be a strong vehicle for delivering codes that analyze AI/ML-based models for explainability. Such explainability and trustworthiness will be essential for R&D applications in regulated spaces such as clean energy systems and climate-mitigation technologies. Trustworthy and transparent workflows for AI/ML models will be necessary to apply those approaches to advanced nuclear energy and integrated energy systems technology R&D, a field which demands high standards of safety and performance. Finally, an ML-based application could be completely trustworthy and explainable and still give the wrong answer; more precisely, the answer has both known and unknown limits. Known limits are probabilities of correctness, and some AI/ML methods (such as reinforcement learning) benefit from continual training and supervision. Collecting feedback on correct versus incorrect outputs needs to be coordinated. AI/ML software deployed into gateways, as opposed to running in separate, isolated environments by each user, can track each methods' success rates.

6.5 Usability and user experience

Using gateways to enhance usability and the user (and researcher) experience has probably received the least amount of attention by the field. The application of AI/ML methods within gateways to enhance user experience (such as guided access, usage analytics, digital assistants) would enhance science gateways' capabilities and advance the field to a new level of maturity. In this space, we expect Javascript-based AI/ML solutions to become important for gateways. Already, there is a vibrant ecosystem of such frameworks, including: TensorFlow.js[1], ml5.js[2], Propel[3], Brain.js,[4] ml.js,[5] Neuro.js,[6] Synaptic,[7] and others. Worthy of mention, also, is ConvNetJS[8] which has some particularly user-friendly educational web applications. We note that AI has already begun to shape a lot of human/machine interfaces. Google search can know and categorize images from text. Voice assistants have become good at parsing queries and returning data correctly. We expect AI to transform Science Gateways themselves, as well as the way they work. "The main trick here is to allow humans to stay human. For decades computers were not exciting to use as they required us to change our ways."—Heilmann.[9] Gateways were always trying to help the humans stay human, AI/ML should enable them to succeed in new ways.

6.6 AI for gateway cyberinfrastructure

In addition to opportunities to leverage AI/ML in research, there are also benefits to adopting these technologies in the underlying cyberinfrastructure powering the

---

1 https://www.tensorflow.org/js

2 https://ml5js.org/

3 https://stackshare.io/propel

4 https://github.com/BrainJS/brain.js

5 https://github.com/mljs/ml

6 https://neuro.js.org/

7 http://caza.la/synaptic/#/

8 https://cs.stanford.edu/people/karpathy/convnetjs/

9 https://www.infoq.com/news/2018/11/human-interfaces-ai/

gateways. For, instance, there are opportunities for centralizing sets of services that could be leveraged for small/short computational jobs (such as classifying an item) that could be provided by frameworks such as Tapis [49], Airavata [50], HUBzero [51], or even commercial cloud services (AWS lambda etc.) with potential to support a hosted catalog of AI/ML functions that could be leveraged by existing and new gateways. Gateways could leverage these lambda-like functions for AI integrations both for AI/ML research as well as incorporating some of these tools into the way the gateway is managed and delivers functionality—recommendations, analyzing gateway data/metrics, and classification of user jobs/workflows that could make gateway operations more efficient and useful to end users/researchers. Further, there is the potential for gateways to leverage AI to enhance usability and accessibility through

- Chatbots—gateways could support customers in real-time and also help reduce help service costs as leveraging AI instead of manual support. These AI chatbots could learn from researcher responses and offer better support with every day and iteration. Additionally, this can also translate to more sustainability as operations run with less staff focus on this and the ability to focus more on gateway functions.

- Accessibility compliance—automated scanning can provide gateway accessibility solutions that will audit gateway interfaces for accessibility. This allows gateway developers to always have the gateway Americans with Disabilities Act (ADA) and Web Content Accessibility Guidelines (WCAG) compliant.

- Better search with natural language processing (NLP)—a large element that can impact usability is search. When users perform searches on gateway, they are looking for something specific. Using semantic search, can make their experience more user-friendly and rewarding and allow them to utilize the gateway better and continue to use it, increasing retention.

- AI research assistants and personalized user experiences—AI-powered assistants are becoming increasingly popular in the world of e-commerce, and there is large potential for these AI-powered virtual assistants to assist gateway users and helping them out in their research journey.

- Sentiment analysis of user correspondence—AI-driven sentiment analysis tools can aid in precisely understanding how researchers feel about services and features. Such tools can analyze researcher correspondence and comments to provide a precise overview of the likeability of the current gateway. This data can help gateway managers/developers improve offerings, add new features, remove unwanted features, and offer a better user experience, leading to increased research outputs, retention, and potential growth and sustainability.

- Cybersecurity—AI-driven pattern recognition of bad actor behaviors can analyze system access and activities to aid in identification of compromised accounts or API security flaws. This type of data and recommendations can assist gateway and infrastructure providers in identifying and addressing security vulnerabilities leading to better protection of this advanced computing and data resources and research intellectual property. We go into more detail in the next section for this topic.

Overall, AI will be revolutionary in the way gateways can be developed/managed/protected and how users will interact with the gateway. Investing in and developing AI-powered tools is a concrete area that will lead to improvements in gateway usability and functionality and doing so in centralized ways can push the entire research community forward.

7. Cybersecurity and critical infrastructure protection

The primary danger posed by the use of Science Gateways comes from the "community account" model on which these applications are based. Some of the science gateway frameworks create on purpose a single account through which they schedule all the jobs by a group of users of the web-facing interface, for example, [6] allowing for accessing HPC resources nationwide in the USA.

Because it is automated, such systems must submit their jobs (typically) without going through two-factor authentication systems (although the gateway infrastructure could, in principle use a two-factor system on the web-facing side). HUBzero has implemented such modules and allows for re-use of login credentials such as Google accounts only if the two-factor system is used at least once during the first login to the system.

Science gateway frameworks are differently designed in regard to security: some only run a limited set of commands related to moving files and a science code, others such as Jupyter Notebooks take code from a web-facing interface and run it on the target system.

Most of the science codes developed in research domains are often written without any kind of security in mind. AI networks themselves, depending on the details of their training, could, in principle, contain vulnerabilities that would be very hard to identify. Individual applications are likely to have numerous vulnerabilities and a clever hacker could provide input parameter files that trigger buffer overrun attacks, etc. In addition, there is the small (but nonvanishing) chance that the science gateway framework itself might be hacked in some way.

Some solutions help mitigating these issues, for example, singularity with AppArmor on the target system. AppArmor provides kernel-level protection against arbitrary sorts of unwanted access. AI is a promising solution *via* pattern recognition of bad actor behaviors supporting to identify compromised accounts or API security flaws.

8. Outlook

Outreach to different target groups will be a crucial topic to establish new science gateways in addition to the ones already used in the AI/ML community. Zooniverse is a great example of a science gateway for collaborating on AI methods. It is one of the frameworks we plan to reach out to. The academic community is well reachable at conferences, and thus, presenting about science gateways and AI at a diverse set of conferences can connect the communities. Furthermore, federal funding programs for AI/ML research and development are important influencers in this space. NSF, NASA, Advanced Research Project Agency-Energy (ARPA-E), Office of Nuclear Energy (DOE-NE) and Office of Energy Efficiency & Renewable Energy (DOE-EERE) all have solicitations associated with AI/ML applications. The last three of these agencies are in the energy space. Existing science gateways in the AI area are good starting points to analyze the uptake of such gateways by the community and to identify existing pain points using such solutions. Partnering with industry is a promising way to accelerate the collaboration between the science gateways and the AI/ML community. The goal is not only to increase the uptake of science gateways for AI methods but also to increase the uptake of AI methods for science gateway infrastructures. Both fields can benefit from each other and accelerate science *via* combining methods for ML with usability of science gateways. Integrating science gateways into teaching will further enhance the knowledge in the community and train students on using and potentially developing science gateways and/or AI/ML concepts and methods and, hence, train the next generation of users and developers. With AI being such an important field in academia and industry, this is a crucial step for highly needed workforce development. This combination of AI/ML and science gateways creates the next generation of critical infrastructure for research and teaching.

Acknowledgements

The authors would like to acknowledge SGCI and NSF as funding body for SGCI's funding under award 1547611. B.M. Villegas Martínez would like to thank finantial support of the Mexican National Council on Science and Technology (CONACyT) through the postdoctoral scholarship CVU 549550. Wilmer Contreras Sepulveda would like to thank CONACyT for the academic scholarship to develop master studies.

Author details

Sandra Gesing[1*], Marlon Pierce[2], Suresh Marru[2], Michael Zentner[3], Kathryn Huff[4], Shannon Bradley[5], Sean B. Cleveland[6], Steven R. Brandt[7], Rajiv Ramnath[8], Kerk Kee[9], Maytal Dahan[10], Braulio M. Villegas Martínez[11], Wilmer Contreras Sepulveda[11] and José J. Sánchez Mondragón[11]

1 Applied R&D, University of Illinois Systems Discovery Partners Institute, US

2 Cyberinfrastructure Integration Research Center, Indiana University, US

3 Sustainable Scientific Software Division, San Diego Supercomputer Center, US

4 Department of Nuclear, Plasma and Radiological, University of Illinois at Urbana-Champaign, US

5 Innovative Software and Data Analysis, University of Illinois at Urbana-Champaign, US

6 Information Technology Services Cyberinfrastructure, University of Hawaiʻi, US

7 Computer Science and Engineering, Louisiana State University, US

8 Computer Science and Engineering, The Ohio State University, US

9 College of Media and Communication, Texas Tech University, US

10 Advanced Computing Interfaces, Texas Advanced Computing Center, US

11 Optics Department, National Institute of Astrophysics, Optics and Electronics, Mexico

*Address all correspondence to: sgesing@uillinois.edu

IntechOpen

© 2023 The Author(s). Licensee IntechOpen. This chapter is distributed under the terms of the Creative Commons Attribution License (http://creativecommons.org/licenses/by/3.0), which permits unrestricted use, distribution, and reproduction in any medium, provided the original work is properly cited.

References

[1] RDA VRE-IG. https://www.rd-alliance.org/groups/vre-ig.html. [Online; Accessed: 09 March 2021]

[2] Gesing S, Brandt S, Bradley S, Potkewitz M, Kee K, Whysel N, Perri M, Cleveland S, Rugg A, Smith J. A vision for science gateways: bridging the gap and broadening the outreach. In: Practice and Experience in Advanced Research Computing, PEARC '21, New York, NY, USA, 2021. Boston, MA, USA, Association for Computing Machinery

[3] AI4Mars. https://www.zooniverse.org/projects/hiro-ono/ai4mars. [Online; Accessed: 09 March 2021]

[4] Zooniverse. https://www.zooniverse.org/. [Online; Accessed: 09 March 2021]

[5] Gesing S, Zentner M, Clark S, Stirm C, Haley B. Hubzero®: novel concepts applied to established computing infrastructures to address communities' needs. In: Proceedings of the Practice and Experience in Advanced Research Computing on Rise of the Machines (Learning), PEARC '19, New York, NY, USA, 2019. Chicago, IL, USA, Association for Computing Machinery

[6] Pierce M, Marru S, Abeysinghe E, Pamidighantam S, Christie M, Wannipurage D. Supporting science gateways using apache airavata and scigap services. In: Proceedings of the Practice and Experience on Advanced Research Computing, PEARC '18, New York, NY, USA, 2018. Pittsburgh, PA, USA, Association for Computing Machinery

[7] Padhy S, Jamthe A, Cleveland SB, Smith JA, Stubbs J, Garcia C, Packard M, Terry S, Looney J, Cardone R, Dahan M, Jacobs GA. Building tapis v3 streams api support for real-time streaming data event-driven workflows. In: Practice and Experience in Advanced Research Computing, PEARC '21, New York, NY, USA, 2021. Boston, MA, USA, Association for Computing Machinery

[8] Gateways Conferences. https://sciencegateways.org/engage/annual-conference. [Online; Accessed: 09 March 2021]

[9] PEARC Conference. https://pearc.acm.org/. [Online; Accessed 09 March 2021]

[10] eScience Conference. https://escience2021.org/. [Online; Accessed: 09 March 2021]

[11] SC Conference Series - The International Conference for High Performance Computing, Networking, Storage, and Analysis. https://supercomputing.org/. [Online; Accessed: 09 March 2021]

[12] The 8th International Online & Onsite Conference on Machine Learning, Optimization, and Data Science. https://lod2022.icas.cc/. [Online; Accessed: 09 March 2021]

[13] Atkinson M, Gesing S. IWSG 2018 - International Workshop on Science Gateways 2018. CEUR Workshop Proceedings: IWSG; 2019

[14] NSF AI Institutes. https://www.nsf.gov/pubs/2020/nsf20604/nsf20604.htm. [Online; Accessed: 09 March 2021]

[15] NSF OAC. https://www.nsf.gov/cise/oac/about.jsp. [Online; Accessed 09 March 2021]

[16] The National Artificial Intelligence Research and Development Strategic Plan - 2019 update. https://www.nitrd.

gov/pubs/National-AI-RD-Strategy-2019.pdf. [Online; Accessed: 09 March 2021]

[17] 3 questions about the Amazon–National Science Foundation collaboration on fairness in AI. https://www.amazon.science/3-questions-about-the-amazon-national-science-foundation-collaboration-on-fairness-in-ai. [Online; Accessed: 09 March 2021]

[18] Turing AM. Computing Machinery and Intelligence. Netherlands, Dordrecht: Springer; 2009. pp. 23-65

[19] McCulloch W, Pitts W. A logical calculus of the ideas immanent in nervous activity. The Bulletin of Mathematical Biophysics. 1943;**5**(4): 115-133

[20] Towns J, Cockerill T, Dahan M, Foster I, Gaither K, Grimshaw A, et al. Xsede: accelerating scientific discovery. Computing in Science & Engineering. 2014;**16**(05):62-74

[21] Pordes R, Petravick D, Kramer B, Olson D, Livny M, Roy A, et al. The open science grid. Journal of Physics: Conference Series. 2007;**78**:012057

[22] Abadi M, Barham P, Chen J, Chen Z, Davis A, Dean J, et al. Tensorflow: a system for large-scale machine learning. In: Proceedings of the 12th USENIX Conference on Operating Systems Design and Implementation, OSDI'16, pp. 265–283, USA, 2016. Savannah, GA, USA, USENIX Association

[23] The National Artificial Intelligence Research and Development Strategic Plan 2016. https://www.nitrd.gov/PUBS/national_ai_rd_strategic_plan.pdf. [Online; Accessed: 09 March 2021]

[24] The National Artificial Intelligence Research and Development Progress Report. https://www.whitehouse.gov/wp-content/uploads/2019/11/AI-Research-and-Development-Progress-Report-2016-2019.pdf. [Online; accessed 09-03-2021]

[25] Artificial Intelligence (AI) at NSF. https://nsf.gov/cise/ai.jsp. [Online; Accessed: 09 March 2021]

[26] DARPA AI Next Campaign. https://www.darpa.mil/work-with-us/ai-next-campaign. [Online; Accessed: 09-03-2021]

[27] NIH Artificial Intelligence, Machine Learning, and Deep Learning. https://www.nibib.nih.gov/research-funding/machine-learning. [Online; Accessed: 09 March 2021]

[28] DOE Artificial Intelligence and Technology Office. https://www.energy.gov/science-innovation/artificial-intelligence-and-technology-office. [Online; Accessed: 09 March 2021]

[29] Gil Y, Selman B. A 20-Year Community Roadmap for Artificial Intelligence Research in the US. Computing Community Consortium (CCC) and Association for the Advancement of Artificial Intelligence (AAAI). 2019. arXiv preprint arXiv: 1908.02624. Available at: https://cra.org/ccc/resources/workshopreports/

[30] Stone P, Brooks R, Brynjolfsson E, Calo R, Etzioni O, Hager G, et al. Artificial Intelligence and Life in 2030. One hundred year study on artificial intelligence: Report of the 2015-2016 Study Panel. Stanford University, Stanford, CA, p. 2016, 2016

[31] Lawrence KA, Zentner M, Wilkins-Diehr N, Wernert JA, Pierce M, Marru S, et al. Science gateways today and tomorrow: positive perspectives of nearly 5000 members of the research community. Concurrency and

Computation: Practice and Experience. 2015;**27**(16):4252-4268

[32] Wilkinson MD, Dumontier M, Aalbersberg IJJ, Appleton G, Axton M, Baak A, et al. The FAIR Guiding Principles for scientific data management and stewardship. Scientific Data. 2016 Mar 15;**3**:160018. DOI: 10.1038/sdata.2016.18. Erratum in: Sci Data. 2019 Mar 19;6(1):6. PMID: 26978244; PMCID: PMC4792175. Available from: https://pubmed.ncbi.nlm.nih.gov/26978244/

[33] Project at the intersecion of AI and physics. http://www.ncsa.illinois.edu/news/story/\doe_awards_2.2m_to_project_at_the_intersection_of_ai_and_high_energy_physic. [Online; Accessed: 09 March 2021]

[34] Collaborative Research: Frameworks: Machine learning and FPGA computing for real-time applications in big-data physics experiments. https://figshare.com/articles/poster/\Collaborative_Research_Frameworks_Machine_Learning_and_FPGA_computing_for_real-time_applications_in_big-data_physics_experiments/11803764. [Online; Accessed: 09 March 2021]

[35] Akiyama K, Alberdi A, Alef W, Asada K, Azulay R, Baczko A-K, et al. First M87 event horizon telescope results. IV. Imaging the central supermassive black hole. The Astrophysical Journal Letters. 2019; **875**(1):L4

[36] Shi B, Calabretta N, Stabile R. Numerical simulation of an inp photonic integrated cross-connect for deep neural networks on chip. Applied Sciences. 2020;**10**(2):474. DOI: 10.3390/app10020474

[37] Ahmed S, Sánchez Muñoz C, Nori F, Kockum AF. Classification and reconstruction of optical quantum states with deep neural networks. Physical Review Research. 2021;**3**: 033278

[38] Bhusal N, Lohani S, You C, Hong M, Fabre J, Zhao P, et al. Spatial mode correction of single photons using machine learning. Advanced Quantum Technologies. 2021;**4**(3):2000103

[39] You C, Quiroz-Juárez MA, Lambert A, Bhusal N, Dong C, Perez-Leija A, et al. Identification of light sources using machine learning. Applied Physics Reviews. 2020;**7**(2): 021404

[40] AGNet. http://www.ncsa.illinois.edu/about/fellows_awardees/\agnet_weighing_black_holes_with_deep_learning. [Online; Accessed: 09 March 2021]

[41] Agriculture. https://calendars.illinois.edu/detail/6824/33401360. [Online; Accessed: 09 March 2021]

[42] Animal husbandry. https://ai.ncsa.illinois.edu/research/funded-projects/. [Online; Accessed: 09 March 2021]

[43] Food security. https://science-council.food.gov.uk/sites/default/\files/appofadvancedanalyticsfinalreport.pdf. [Online; Accessed: 09 March 2021]

[44] Liljedahl AK, Jones BM, Brubaker M, Budden AE, Cervenec JM, Grosse G, Jones MB, Marini L, McHenry K, Moss J, Morin PJ, Nitze I, Soliman A, Wind G, Witharana C. Permafrost discovery gateway: a web platform to enable discovery and knowledge-generation of permafrost big imagery products. In: AGU Fall Meeting 2019, San Francisco, USA, December 2019. AGU

[45] Infrastructure Deserts. https://storymaps.arcgis.com/stories/\7b8c

2029e30749449a3a692451e51ddf. [Online; Accessed: 09 March 2021]

[46] Wang Z, Christie MA, Abeysinghe E, Chu T, Marru S, Pierce M, and Danko CG. Building a science gateway for processing and modeling sequencing data via apache airavata. In: Proceedings of the Practice and Experience on Advanced Research Computing, pp. 1–7. 2018

[47] Zhou J, Smith K, Wilsbacher G, Sagona P, Reddy D, and Torkian B. Building science gateways for humanities. In: Practice and Experience in Advanced Research Computing, pp. 327–332. 2020

[48] Jia Y, Shelhamer E, Donahue J, Karayev S, Long J, Girshick R, Guadarrama S, Darrell T. Caffe: convolutional architecture for fast feature embedding. In: Proceedings of the 22nd ACM international conference on Multimedia, pp. 675–678, 2014

[49] Cleveland SB, Jamthe A, Padhy S, Stubbs J, Packard M, Looney J, et al. Tapis api development with python: best practices in scientific rest api implementation: Experience implementing a distributed stream api. In: Practice and Experience in Advanced Research Computing, PEARC '20, pp. 181–187, New York, NY, USA, 2020. Portland, OR, USA, Association for Computing Machinery

[50] Marru S, Gunathilake L, Herath C, Tangchaisin P, Pierce M, Mattmann C, et al. Apache airavata: a framework for distributed applications and computational workflows. In: Proceedings of the 2011 ACM Workshop on Gateway Computing Environments, GCE '11, pp. 21–28, New York, NY, USA, 2011. Seattle, Washington, USA, Association for Computing Machinery

[51] David Benham and Sandra Gesing. Hubzero© goes onescienceplace: The next community-driven steps for providing software-as-a-service. In: 2019 15th International Conference on eScience (eScience), pp. 642–643, 2019

Section 3

Sustainable and Digital Twin-Based Approaches for the Transport Infrastructure

Chapter 5

Providing Sustainable Transport Infrastructure through Internalization of External Costs: A Case Study from South-Eastern European Countries

Christina Nikolova

Abstract

The most important goals for transport systems development in the European countries are related to increasing transport system efficiency and sustainability and pushing national economies' competitiveness. After a thorough analysis of transport costs, a system of measures should be undertaken to achieve these goals. All these issues are on the top of the political agenda so far, considering the impacts of the COVID pandemic in recent years and the current developments of Just Transition and the European Green Deal ambitions. However, they could not be reached without accounting for transport's social costs, especially external ones. The chapter's main objective is to demonstrate the opportunities of the internalization approach and its updates for evaluating marginal external transport costs on a national level for South-Eastern European countries. As a result, a background will be provided to help policymakers in these counties to prioritize measures and projects envisaged in inland modes of transport based on potential savings for the society, which is not done so far. The chapter also discusses the effects of improving transport infrastructure functioning and performance by using internalization of external costs.

Keywords: sustainable transport, external costs for transport, internalization of external costs, infrastructure charging, transport policy

1. Introduction

The main ambition of the Transport policy in the EU is to provide efficient and sustainable transport systems and services to societies and to push national economies' competitiveness. These goals could be reached through a system of measures undertaken after a thorough analysis of transport costs [1]. However, this analysis needs the application of contemporary cost accounting approaches in transport and up-to-date infrastructure charging principles.

The infrastructure charging system in transport in the EU is based on the "user is to pay" principle. However, besides the internal costs (private costs) calculated in infrastructure charges, other costs are generally not reflected in charges but influence external parties. Hence, it is necessary to differentiate charges to account for external costs for different modes of transport. The differentiation could be achieved by internalizing external costs for transport in infrastructure charges by applying a common approach for infrastructure charging in all modes of transport.

All these issues appear to be of utmost importance when analyzing transport activities and the opportunities for funding infrastructure projects in South-Eastern European Countries and to achieve respective transport policy goals.

The evaluation of marginal external transport costs on a national level for South-Eastern European countries is suggested in this chapter to clarify the application of the approach and its opportunities to balance transport modes sustainably. Furthermore, the results could help countries' policymakers prioritize measures and projects envisaged in inland modes of transport based on potential savings for society, which has not been done so far. Finally, the chapter suggests measures for improving transport infrastructure funding and performance.

2. Methodology for evaluation of external infrastructure costs

On the European level, many projects and studies were carried out to estimate the proper impact of externalities and to translate it into societal costs (GRACE, UNITE, RECORDIT, SPECTRUM, HEATCO, NEWEXT, etc.). Although the transferability of results remains limited, a considerable number of different researchers pave the way toward proper valuation. The Handbook on the external costs of transport and its updates give a detailed overview of what is being done in the field of cost estimation so far [2].

The cost data used by infrastructure companies are insufficient, heterogeneous, and inappropriate for thorough analysis and evaluation. On the other hand, using complex cost categories and new information sources is a resource- and time-intensive, which is unacceptable in the short term [3]. Therefore, existing practices and methods for determining infrastructure charges are the initial basis for specifying cost categories and the data used for estimating marginal social costs for transport [4].

The necessity to develop a common framework for charging for transport infrastructure use is defined at the European Union level [5]. It is because infrastructure charges affect the conditions of competition in the internal market. Furthermore, they are related to ensuring access to the transport market and significantly affect the development of international transport [6]. Therefore, in order to achieve the objectives set, the following basic principles are justified:

- The same basic principles are applied to all modes of transport;

- Levying infrastructure charges lead to greater efficiency of the use of transport infrastructure.

- All users must pay for the costs they cause, or at least ensure that operating costs are covered;

- The charges must be directly linked to the costs induced by infrastructure users and other costs, including the environmental and other external costs.

- They must differ only where there are fundamental differences in the cost and quality of services and should not be discriminatory regarding users' nationality and origin.

The only approach that fully meets these criteria is charging based on marginal social costs, i.e., users pay the costs (internal and external) that they trigger when using the infrastructure. This approach incentivizes consumers to reduce infrastructure costs while maximizing individual benefits and economic and social well-being.

Besides the costs reflected in the applied infrastructure charges (internal costs), some costs are not paid by the users causing them but affect parties external to the transport process and are not included in the charges [2]. Some of these external costs are marginal. The procedures for allocating costs depend on the valuation method applied. Cost allocation is usually done indirectly through theoretical and empirical cost analysis, using different indicators and coefficients of the other influencing factors [7]; these allocation indices can be combined to establish marginal costs for different vehicle types [6]. The allocation indices can be combined to evaluate marginal costs for different vehicle types.

The introduction of proper charging for the use of transport infrastructure provides for charges to be set entirely based on full social costs, i.e., variable and fixed infrastructure costs and external costs [8]. To this end, it is necessary to specify how to assess the different types of external costs. In doing so, their calculation is again linked to the setting of marginal costs.

Three major groups of external costs could be specified as follows:

1. *Congestion costs* – incl. Costs for the scarcity of infrastructure, including time and additional operating costs; for scheduled transport: delay costs as well as additional costs in urban areas – including time losses of non-motorized traffic in urban areas;

2. *Environmental costs* – incl. *Costs for air pollution* [9], – health/medical costs, crop losses, building damages etc.; *costs for climate change* – avoidance costs to reduce risk of climate change and damage costs of increasing average temperature; noise costs –annoyance and health costs; *well-to-tank costs* – including climate change and air pollution costs of energy consumption and GHG emissions of up- and downstream processes, cost elements such as repair cost and restoration measures (e.g. unsealing, renaturation, green bridges); *costs for habitat damage* – including damage or restoration costs of air pollutant related biodiversity losses [10]; and *costs for soil and water pollution* – including restoration and repair costs for soil and water pollutant with focus on transport-related heavy metal and hydrocarbon emissions; *noise costs* – including the environmental price of noise that reflects the welfare loss occurring with one extra decibel of noise as well as induced annoyance and health costs.

3. *Accident costs* – including medical costs, production losses, and losses of human lives.

In assessing the *congestion costs*, three leading indicators are used that affect the level of these costs – the assessment of the travel time, the ratio of " travel time – demand for transport services," and the function of demand. The value of travel time can be evaluated in several different ways: first, by assessing the value of time for society as a whole. In this case, a distinction should be made between the time to work and the rest spent on travel. The salary per hour may reflect the production result that can be achieved for the time used for transport [11].

Concerning rest time, the willingness to pay for actual or hypothetical consumer preferences should be assessed. These preferences are studied using surveys. The assessment of private travel is carried out using the neoclassical model of individuals maximizing the utility of the consumption of services under certain budgetary constraints [12]. The costs for business trips take into account individual aspects of a person's productivity. Further research is needed in this area to justify better the indicators that determine the assessment of the travel time.

The optimal level of congestion charges is determined by the intersection of the cost curve of transport infrastructure users and the demand curve for transport services. This level reflects the demand for access to transport infrastructure and responds to the necessity of internalizing these costs in the charges, thus providing for cost reduction. Thus, the demand function determines the relationship between actual external costs and equilibrium charges to address the consequences of congestion.

The flow of vehicles providing transport services can be explained as a physical relationship between the number of vehicles using the transport infrastructure over a specified period and the corresponding speed at which those vehicles move. The ratio of "travel time – demand for transport services" can be described with different functions (hyperbolic, logit, linear) [8]. In this case, it is crucial to consider the relative share of demand diverted due to congestion, which will be directed to another time or alternative route.

A significant factor influencing the occurrence of congestion is the costs of individual infrastructure users. These costs increase as the number of users increases. Thus, if the charges paid by users are set to reflect the actual external congestion costs, the demand for access will be reduced and, together with it, the external costs themselves.

Several studies have been carried out in the EU on external congestion costs. However, these congestion impacts have not been sufficiently investigated [13]. Moreover, it is unclear whether these costs should be defined as external when scheduled services are offered. For example, the costs associated with delays due to congestion caused by one rail operator to another are external. However, it is debatable whether delays in the presence of only one operator should be considered essential for price fixing or included in them. With this in mind and based on the conclusions on the state and use of infrastructure in different modes of transport, it can be summarized that these costs must be considered when determining infrastructure charges for road and air transport and are less critical in rail. In this respect, it is necessary to study them further and include them in the charges when reaching the appropriate level of use of the infrastructure.

The *environmental costs* are related to eliminating heterogeneous transport influences such as noise, air, water, and soil pollution. However, the valuation of these influences is hampered by the fact that it is not goods and services that can be sold and bought. Therefore, different methods are used [14], such as:

- the market for substitute goods and services, respectively, transport costs where consumers benefit from public recreational facilities, are used to estimate these costs. Alternatively, they could be evaluated by using the consumer assessment of individual goods and services depending on their exposure to pollution or noise. Thus, assessing such goods and services concerning their environmental characteristics can be used. The environmental costs can also be assessed by examining the members of society willing to pay to reduce or eliminate adverse environmental effects. There are some difficulties associated with the sensitivity of individuals to the ecological factor in applying this method;

- conditional estimates – this method is related to a study of consumers' willingness to pay in order to eliminate adverse effects or their willingness to pay in order to continue to tolerate these effects. The difficulties relate to questionnaires development and the provision of credible answers, as well as to psychological biases associated with a lower willingness to pay for the elimination of harmful influences than to accept benefits in order to continue to bear them;

- indirect methods are applicable for the costs of preventing environmental pollution. They are applied in two stages: the first is technical. It aims to quantify the consequences of adverse environmental effects. The second is to assess the damage caused, both through the market prices of the damaged goods and through the repair costs of such damage or other subjective assessments. However, the application of this method involves difficulties due to the lack of information, and the value of environmental damage is inaccurate.

Measuring the different adverse effects is complex, but there are still some studies [15] attempting to quantify them accurately. For example, noise is measured depending on the duration and sensitivity of the human ear. Its impacts are usually assessed by lowering the prices of buildings in noisier areas. Noise also impacts people's health due to its influence on the cardiovascular system and sleep, which are general health components. Air pollution is measured by the amounts of harmful vehicle emissions – nitrogen and sulfur oxides, particulate matter, and volatile organic compounds. Assessing their impact on people, animals, plants, and buildings is complicated. There are still significant inconsistencies in determining the long-term effect of these on human health. The values estimates include the direct costs of disability, the cost of protection from emissions, and the assessment of consumers' willingness to pay to avoid damage caused by air pollution.

The *accident costs* are inherent in the transport industry [16]. They have a high value depending on the number of people killed and injured in accidents, the cost of human life, or the damage caused. The value of human life is most often assessed by assessing human capital and calculating losses or reduced production due to damage caused. It is also possible to assess the willingness to pay extra for transport at greater risk.

For the calculation of the accident costs, it is necessary to consider not only the assessment of the value of human life but also the value of the damage caused to persons and property, as well as the production losses resulting from the absence of employees from work. The cost of the damage includes direct (medical expenses, transport of victims, etc.), indirect costs (loss of production), and subjective assessments (of pain and suffering). Therefore, it is impossible to determine to what extent these costs are covered by transport insurance [12]. Furthermore, there are also fluctuations in the extent to which these external costs are related to the transport volume, respectively, with the flow of vehicles and at driving speeds. These issues also require studying the interaction between congestion and the number of transport accidents.

The possibilities for internalizing external costs are not yet fully used in the infrastructure charging systems in transport sectors of the South-Eastern European countries [6]. Except for charges on liquid fuels and excise duties relating to covering the costs of protecting and preventing environmental pollution, there are only a few to consider these costs (for example, environmental and noise-related markups in airport charges). Therefore, there is a need for in-depth and concrete research into these opportunities and the definition of approaches and methods for evaluating external costs and their internalization in infrastructure charges. Furthermore, the revenues from such charges may be used to finance future investments. There is no need to set a uniform approach to measuring external costs, but it must be determined how different cost estimates or approaches can be applied correctly. However, the possibilities for internalizing external costs can be determined by whether the marginal cost function is increasing or decreasing [17]. Therefore, determining the marginal costs of transport infrastructure should be based on the average of the elasticity factors of maintenance and repair costs to changes in transport volume.

Thus, if the cost function is decreasing, as in rail and waterborne transport, the marginal costs have not reached their minimum, and there are opportunities for economies of scale. That is, with a 1% increase in transport volume, costs increased by less than 1%. Therefore, in this case, it is possible to apply supplements and include external costs in infrastructure charges without drastically reducing revenue. Conversely, when the cost function is increasing, i.e., a 1% increase in transport volume corresponds to a more significant cost increase, there is a decreasing return on a scale. In this case, the inclusion of external costs will cause a substantial increase in charges and affect the usage of transport infrastructure.

The discussed charging approach is critical to ensure the efficient use of infrastructure and creates the conditions for its financing from users' payments, which require new and different funding models. Transport operators and users paying the actual costs have clear incentives to make their choice, for example:

- To use vehicles that cause less damage to the infrastructure, less environmental pollution, and are more secure;

- To rearrange their routes and logistics chains to those with lower infrastructure damage levels, less congestion, lower risk of accidents, and a lower environmental impact;

- To reconsider their modal choice and use modes of transport with fewer external effects.

Consequently, the infrastructure charging system developed in implementing such a common approach provides incentives to improve transport performance through more comprehensive benefits by reducing the costs associated with external effects. Even transport operators who have not changed their services will benefit from changes undertaken by others, such as reducing congestion and improving infrastructure conditions, reducing the risk of accidents, etc.

3. Methodology for internalization of external costs

Based on the analysis carried out of the current principles of infrastructure charges in transport, it is found that the charges in the different modes of transport are based on the average or marginal cost of maintaining, repairing, and operating the infrastructure concerned [1]. Therefore, to take into account marginal social costs for transport, general principles for evaluating costs, including external ones, should apply to all modes of transport.

Cost grouping is essential as it reflects the content of the costs already determined and is a step toward their allocation. At this stage, the existing cost categorization may be used, or accounting information sources adapted to the theory of marginal costs [18]. However, to justify the inclusion of the relevant group of costs in determining infrastructure charges, it is necessary to define more detailed and precise cost categories. In doing so, an account should be taken of the information limitations according to which specific categories of expenditure are aggregated, and it is not possible to accurately reflect the different variable costs [19].

In some cases, determining the reasons for different costs is relatively easy, and in others – not so much. Therefore, the different cost categories may be further grouped according to their reasons. The individual elements of the variable costs shall then be defined using the relevant qualitative technical and economic indicators.

After grouping the costs according to their intended purpose, it is crucial to create the necessary prerequisites for their transfer to those who cause them through the system of infrastructure charges [8]. Ideally, charges should change as each cost changes. However, the practical application of such an approach is not easy, so it is necessary to use more generalized categories. First, an analytical approach may be applied when examining infrastructure costs based on the total costs allocated to one vehicle. The second option is to apply the synthesis approach, which collects information on the costs associated with individual vehicles and summarizes these costs. The availability of data on the costs concerned their categorization and the possibilities for allocating them predetermine the use of one of the two approaches. Synthesis is appropriate when the objective is to determine the function of the total costs from which to infer the first derivative (the function of marginal costs). Where the total costs are known and the individual elements are not, it is more appropriate to use the analysis.

For cost allocation purposes, it is necessary to link the different cost categories to the relevant indicators, using data on physical and technical interaction between vehicles and roads or railways. In applying this approach, the allocation procedure must be transparent. These requirements may be tailored as follows:

When allocating marginal costs depending on the weight and number of vehicles, axle load indicators are used mainly. The mileage indicator is used to allocate costs that do not depend on the gross weight of the vehicles. In order to improve the information base, it is necessary to extend the above analysis method (in terms of mixed traffic, the share of different heavy goods vehicles).

Estimates of individual costs differ; some have a direct financial dimension, others depend on the likelihood of an event, and others have a physical or physiological expression (see **Table 1**).

The focus at this stage should be on the cost drivers and not on the incurrence of the costs themselves. Infrastructure costs, as well as environmental and congestion costs, can be directly attributed to the transport volume [20]. In this regard, the infrastructure charges imposed on consumers are the most appropriate toolbox for ensuring adequate price signals in the transport infrastructure market. However, concerning the costs caused by transport accidents, this toolbox can be assessed as inappropriate. On the other hand, approaches based on general taxation and specific transport taxes and charges (e.g., vehicle tax and charges on liquid fuels) are not particularly precise as they are not based on the specific costs incurred due to transport accidents. Furthermore, these taxes and charges do not alert consumers to correct their behavior because of accidents.

Fixed costs		Variable costs	
Internal costs	**External costs/ benefits**	**Internal costs**	**External costs/benefits**
Capital expenditures:	*Costs:*		*Other external costs*
• return on capital; • interest payments; • -asset regrowth.	• restrictive effects; • pollution of nature; • visual disturbances.		• *Air and water pollution:* (local/local pollutants – e.g., dusting; regional pollutants – e.g., nitrates; global pollutants – e.g., carbon dioxide).
Fixed running costs:	*Benefits:*	*Variable running costs:*	*Costs/Benefits:*
• maintenance costs (weather and climate-related); • operating costs (lighting, traffic management, information); • administration costs.	• improved access; • systemic benefits; • increased productivity.	• operating costs (traffic management, use, ancillary services); • maintenance costs related to operation (reconstruction, replacement of rails, repair).	*Transport accidents* *Congestion* *Noise and vibration*

Table 1.
Costs elements related to the use and maintenance of infrastructure.

Introducing the charges related to externalities will lead to the provision of additional revenue from infrastructure charges. From a fairness point of view, it is desirable to use the accumulated money to compensate victims of accidents, for example, or to finance measures to limit future negative influences. Furthermore, even higher cost recovery levels can be achieved if the funds are allocated to achieve common infrastructure objectives [21]. Analyses carried out on the European level provide a reason to summarize that the total revenues for the transport system will exceed infrastructure costs.

Differentiation of charges taking into account external costs is also possible as different modes of transport have different external costs. Such a measure would more effectively impact the charges for using the infrastructure. In this respect, it is necessary to introduce simultaneously environmental charges related to noise, harmful emissions, transport accidents, and congestion in different modes of transport. Demand for infrastructure capacity changes depending on the hours of the day, the type of traffic, and the direction of alternative routes. In principle, transport operators should pay different fees for different destinations and times of day in order to adequately reflect the insufficient (depleted) capacity and ensure its more efficient allocation [8]. This guideline should be used to increase the efficiency and sustainability of the use of transport infrastructure.

Improving the infrastructure charging system by internalizing external transport costs will lead to more efficient use of infrastructure and higher coverage of the costs of maintaining and operating it. In addition, this process will create prerequisites for financing the construction of new infrastructure. In combination with subsidies provided directly by the state to offset the overall public benefit to non-direct users of infrastructure, a high, or perhaps full, level of covering maintenance and operation costs is likely to be achieved. Suppose full coverage is not ensured, and the state wishes to ensure a higher level. In that case, this can be achieved by imposing additional, fixed, non-discriminatory user charges that do not change the proportions between modes of transport. In addition, investment projects will, at least in the medium term, require a high level of cost coverage. In such cases, higher charges may be applied for a particular time, following the rules on non-discrimination and providing guarantees that monopoly profits will not be allowed to be realized.

In the presence of sufficiently reliable and detailed methodologies based on the described approach, it is possible to recalculate the marginal costs for each year [22]. Thus, in the event of a change in cost ratios or a significant change in the use of infrastructure (e.g., when capacity is exhausted), changes will be able to be reflected promptly and infrastructure charges updated. In this way, they will consider the actual conditions for using the infrastructure and provide adequate revenue for undertakings offering access to it.

However, it should be taken into account that the marginal costs do not change proportionately as the volume of transport changes. Therefore, it cannot be assumed that the mathematical function of the costs is linear. Furthermore, it is necessary to determine what other factors affect the costs of maintaining and operating transport infrastructure. All these limitations require an examination of the type of cost function.

3.1 Evaluation of marginal costs function

Research carried out at the European level has shown that the main costs, which vary according to the volume of transport for railways and road infrastructure, are the cost of maintenance and repair. The leading indicators used to allocate costs are defined in this respect. For terminal infrastructures, such as airports and ports, these are the labor costs of staff engaged in servicing aircraft/vessels and passengers or handling goods [22]. In road and rail transport, the leading indicators are the volume of traffic in gross tonne-kilometers, the number of bridges and tunnels, the level of electrification, and the infrastructure's operation duration. Regarding terminal infrastructure, the airports and ports shall consider the number of air movements, passengers served, and ships served. Seasonal and weekly fluctuations in transport volume should also not be overlooked.

The function describing the change in the cost of maintaining and repairing the transport infrastructure presents the relationship between these costs and the transport volume. For the definition of this heading, the relationship between the total marginal costs of transport infrastructure (TC_{infra}), the volume of traffic (Q), and the factors influencing them should be clarified. Influencing factors may be, for example, infrastructure parameters (I), the cost of construction of the infrastructure (p), vehicle weight (W), speed of movement (S), weather conditions (Z), etc. Therefore, the overall type of cost function suggested by the author is:

$$TC_{infra} = f\ (Q, p, W, S, I, Z, \ \dots) \tag{1}$$

Research carried out in EU countries gives rise to the transcendental logarithmic function being considered the most accurate for studying infrastructure costs in road and rail transport [23]. It provides possibilities for initial analysis of the total costs and phasing out the function according to the type of infrastructure. Another advantage is that it is a flexible mathematical model that gives good results in studying unknown products or cost functions. This model also meets the requirements of neoclassical economic theory related to the substitution of production factors, economies of scale of production, and technological changes [24]. The limitations of using the transcendental logarithmic function are not significant. They relate only to possible changes in the vehicle technologies in use.

The type of aggregated function adapted to railway infrastructure conditions and the necessary cost data is as follows (adapted and suggested by the author):

$$\ln(C_m) = \alpha 0 + \alpha_l . \ln l + \alpha_k . \ln k_t + \alpha_{Qg} . \ln Q_g + \alpha_{Sw} . \ln S_w + \alpha_{Nt} . \ln N_t + \ln l\left(½\beta_{ll} . \ln l + \beta_{lk} . \ln k_t + \beta_{Qg} . \ln Q_g + \beta_{Sw.l} . \ln S_w + \beta_{Ntl} . \ln N_t\right) + \ln kt\left(½\beta_{ktkt.} \ln kt + \beta_{ktQg} . \ln Q_g + \beta_{Swkt.} \ln S_w + \beta_{Ntkt.} \ln N_t\right) + \ln Qg\left(½\beta_{QgQg.} \ln Q_g + \beta_{NtQg} . \ln N_t\right) + \ln N_t(½\beta_{NtNt} . \ln N_t), \quad (2)$$

Where the dependent variable C_m reflects the costs of maintaining railway infrastructure, and the independent variables are:

l – the length of the railway sections;

k_t – the variable determining the electrification of railway lines;

S_w – the number of arrows in each plot;

Q_g – the gross traffic volume on the relevant section;

N_t – the number of trains passing on the sections for a certain period (e.g., for 1 year);

α_0 – constant;

α – the elasticity coefficient;

β – the correlation factor between the indicators.

Data availability and quality influence costs and are crucial for econometric analysis. In this respect, it is necessary to provide detailed data and adapt them to the regression analysis needs. A similar model is suitable for describing the cost function in road transport. The model includes the cost of repairing and maintaining individual road sections, variables for road category, and annual average daily transport volumes.

Concerning airport infrastructure, an appropriate form for the cost function is cubic, as it best describes the cost dependency on the volume of transport at airports with predominant international traffic. The main indicators to be included in the model are as follows: number of staff (n), respectively, duration of work in person-hours by type of activity, annual cost of carrying out the different types of services (C), number of air movements (m), respectively number of passengers served. The study of the type of cost function for different indicators follows the model (adapted and suggested by the author):

$$C = \beta_0 + \beta_{n1}.n + \beta_{n2}.n^2 + \beta_{n3}.n^3 + \beta_{n4}\, n^4 + \varepsilon_t \quad (3)$$

This model must also consider seasonal and weekly fluctuations in transport volume and differences in service standards. In this way, higher reliability of the analysis can be ensured.

In the short term, facilities' wear and tear costs are not so high for port infrastructure. Therefore, the main costs to be considered in the analysis are the costs of loading and unloading operations and the labor costs of port workers. The model describing the type of cost function may include the following indicators: annual costs of using the port (TC), the quantities of freight passing through the port per year (Q), and the total quantity of goods passing through the port over the entire period (Q_{cum}). It is also possible to include the annual investment costs, the number of persons employed in ships' servicing, and the labor costs for those persons. Studies carried out in EU countries show that the most appropriate form of the function is the logarithmic Cobb-Douglas specification of the type (adapted and suggested by the author):

$$\log TC = \log a + b \log Q + c \log Q_{cum} + d_y \quad (4)$$

In the absence of sufficiently detailed and reliable data for econometric analysis (large statistical rows of at least 50 meanings are required), it should be clarified that the summaries made are theoretically valid but require further practical and applied analyses. In addition, they should present the specific results of the correlation between the change in costs and the factors influencing them.

Implementing the first stages of the described approach provides for basic infrastructure charges for roads, railways, ports, and airports to be defined. However, it should be taken into account that the marginal costs do not account for all variable costs, i.e., they need to be included in infrastructure charges in other ways to ensure higher or even full cost recovery.

The marginal costs of transport infrastructure shall be determined by the use of the econometric models or only by the simple determination of the cost elasticity factors relative to the transport volume. In the absence of a sufficiently detailed database of the cost categories, quantifying the marginal costs of transport infrastructure may be done using the principles for the transfer of research results as recommended by the Handbook on external transport costs [2]. The relevant reference values by cost category shall be selected, and the results obtained using the econometric approach shall be applied.

Following the suggested methodological approach, the next stage for infrastructure charging involves markups' calculation to reflect the external costs for transport and harmonize the infrastructure charging systems in different modes of transport. Then, depending on the indicators included in the study of the cost function and calculated elasticity factors, it is necessary to determine the amount of marginal external costs related to each indicator. Thus, the remaining costs (external) can be allocated based on the marginal costs already allocated.

3.2 Calculation of external marginal costs for SEEC for evaluating markups to infrastructure charges

The calculation of markups to marginal infrastructure costs can be carried out by using the transferring tool for the results of econometric studies as suggested in the Handbook on the external costs of transport [2]. However, detailed data on different indicators for certain road sections or individual infrastructure sites should be considered in this case. The coefficients obtained should not be applied directly. Instead, they should be adapted to the using conditions, the characteristics of the country's infrastructure, and the year of calculation. The calculated cost dependency factors for the transport volume will determine the marginal external costs. The remaining additional costs may be allocated proportionally to predetermined cost dependency factors from the average daily traffic volume per category of vehicles. Overall workflow of the model in terms of input data, model variables and output, is presented in **Figure 1**.

Considering recent updates of the Handbook on external transport costs on the European level [2], there are no projects or studies conducted in most South-Eastern

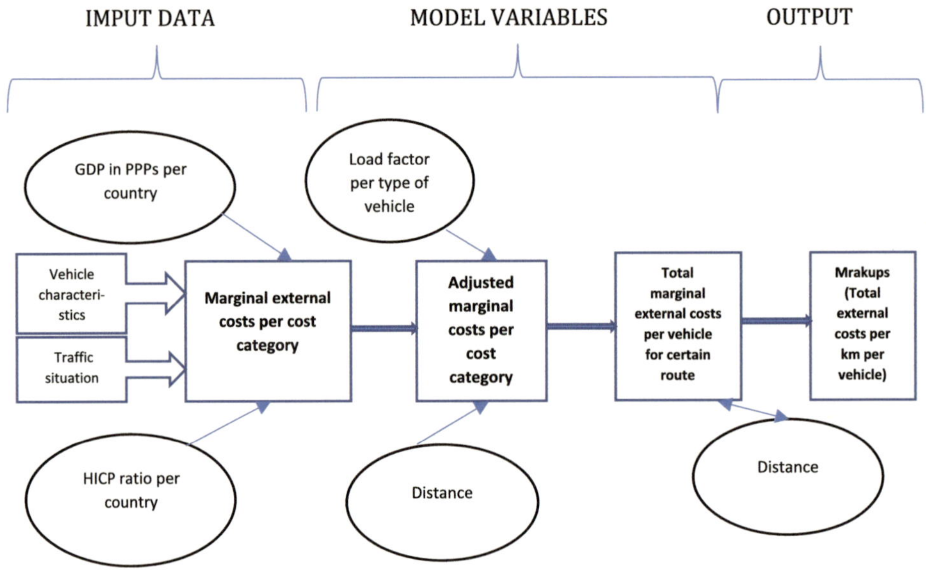

Figure 1.
Model workflow from data input to expected results.

European countries. However, external cost evaluation for some of the countries in this region has been included in the OECD report on external transport costs in Central and Eastern Europe [1]. Still, other relevant studies do not cover most of the SEE region countries.

The Handbook on the external costs of transport represents one of the possible reference bases for further external costs studies in the South-Eastern European countries [25]. The methodology for the external cost calculation can be widely used since the unit values for input figures are presented in monetary terms related to the specific value, such as Euro per hour, per accident, per unit of emission, per life year lost, etc. The output values are presented in a form that can be translated for internalization. The central unit for the infrastructure pricing is the cost per vehicle- or tonne-kilometers. Similar to other studies of external costs, a transfer of cost per passenger or tonne-kilometer has been carried out to compare different modes. Where relevant or valuable, other output unit values are shown. When applying the results to the SEE region, it should be considered that the figures are directly applicable to some SEE countries (EU members). However, for others (non-members), the value transfer approach is used to transfer the data to these countries. It can still provide reliable data for policy purposes at lower accuracy based on the guidelines for estimating external transport costs. The Handbook provides ready estimations with limited case-specific data; total/average and marginal external cost figures are provided for all countries and transport modes. Where relevant, differentiations to relevant vehicle characteristics (e.g., fuel type, size class, etc.) and traffic situation (type of road, day/night, thin/dense traffic, etc.) are provided [2].

The example provided in this section presents the calculations of total marginal external costs for pilot routes in SEE countries (for road and rail infrastructure) by using marginal values in order to present the potential of the described approach to defining markups to marginal infrastructure costs for charging for the use of infrastructure in these countries.

Calculating marginal external costs for specific routes in SEE countries is based on the reference values of the marginal external costs (€ct/vehicle for accident costs and €ct/tkm for all other costs) and transport modes provided by the Handbook referring to 2016.

These values are adjusted by using GDP per capita in PPPs coefficients for 2016 by country and by respective coefficients related to harmonized indices of consumer prices (HICP) for 2021 relative to 2016 (counted to index 2020 = 100). Through this adjustment, the reference values have been updated in line with current economic conditions and reflect the specificities of each SEE country (see **Tables 2** and **3**).

For the approach validation, the calculations of marginal external costs have been made for the pilot routes presented in **Table 4**, which presents the characteristics of each pilot route in detail.

The external costs for pilot routes are calculated according to the recommendations in the Handbook [2] and Annex 2: General instructions for the calculation of external costs [24]. In addition, the following methodology has been applied:

- First, type of vehicle (LDV and HDV), network type (motorways and outside urban), and vkm or tkm for each type of vehicle and section of the network are defined;

- Second, the correct marginal values for external costs by countries (€ct/vkm or tkm) for 2016 from the Handbook on external transport costs are selected and adjusted to 2021, accounting for each SEE country's current economic conditions. It is made by using the coefficient of GDP per capita in PPPs per every SEE country and the HICP ratio for 2021–2016 coefficients (see **Table 2**) as the referent values for marginal accident costs are recommended for the EU as a whole;

- Third, the adjusted marginal values are multiplied by the total volumes (vkm or tkm) to calculate each route's total external costs.

- Thus, the respective external costs for moving vehicles of a particular type on the separate sections and pilot routes are calculated.

- For rail transport, calculations of marginal external costs are made according to the following considerations:

Country	GDP per capita in PPPs coefficient (2016)	Correction factor based on the ratio of HICP (2021–2016)
Bulgaria (BG)	0.49	1.10
Croatia (HR)	0.62	1.07
North Macedonia (NM)	0.37	1.10
Greece (GR)	0.68	1.02
Republic Serbia (RS)	0.39	1.14
Slovenia (SL)	0.84	1.07

Table 2.
Adjustment factors for calculating marginal and total external costs.

External marginal costs	Ref. values €ct/tkm	Adjusted values (€ct/tkm)					
		BG	HR	NM	GR	RS	SL
Road transport							
Accidents (motorways)*	0.25	0.1348	0.1659	0.1018	0.1734	0.1112	0.2247
Congestion							
-LCV							
afternoon peak	10.8	5.821	7.165	4.396	7.491	4.802	9.707
morning peak	37.8	20.374	25.077	15.385	26.218	16.806	33.975
-HDV	66.3	35.74	43.98	26.98	45.99	29.48	59.59
Air pollution							
-LCV							
Gasoline	0.009	0.0049	0.0060	0.0037	0.0062	0.0040	0.0081
Diesel	0.0151	0.0081	0.0100	0.0062	0.0105	0.0067	0.0136
-HGV	0.0061	0.0033	0.0041	0.0025	0.0042	0.0027	0.0041
Noise							
-day	0.01	0.0054	0.0066	0.0041	0.0069	0.0044	0.0090
-night	0.02	0.0108	0.0133	0.0081	0.0139	0.0089	0.0190
Climate change:							
- LCV							
gasoline	1.11	0.5983	0.7364	0.4618	0.7699	0.4935	0.9977
Diesel	1.18	0.6360	0.7828	0.4803	0.8185	0.5246	1.0606
-HDV	0.69	0.3719	0.4578	0.2808	0.4786	0.3068	0.6202
Costs of habitat damage (motorway)							
LCV	1.35	0.7277	0.8956	0.5495	0.9364	0.6002	1.2134
HDV	0.19	0.1024	0.1260	0.0773	0.1318	0.0845	0.1708
Well-to-tank emissions	0.10	0.0539	0.0663	0.0407	0.0694	0.0445	0.0899
Rail transport							
Accidents	0.01	0.0054	0.0066	0.0041	0.0069	0.0044	0.0090
Congestion	0.00	0.00	0.00	0.00	0.00	0.00	0.00
Air pollution							
-electrified	0.004	0.0022	0.0027	0.0016	0.0028	0.0018	0.0036
-non-electrified	0.356	0.1919	0.2362	0.1449	0.2469	0.1583	0.3200
Noise							
-day	0.01	0.0054	0.0066	0.0041	0.0069	0.0044	0.0090
-night	0.02	0.0108	0.0133	0.0081	0.0139	0.0089	0.0190
Climate change:							
-electrified	0.00	0.00	0.00	0.00	0.00	0.00	0.00
-non-electrified	0.087	0.0469	0.0577	0.0354	0.0603	0.0387	0.0782

External marginal costs	Ref. values €ct/tkm	Adjusted values (€ct/tkm)					
		BG	HR	NM	GR	RS	SL
Costs of habitat damage	0.24	0.1294	0.1592	0.0977	0.1734	0.1067	0.2157
Well-to-tank emissions	0.11	0.0593	0.0730	0.0448	0.0763	0.0489	0.0989

*Note: * The external costs for accidents are calculated based on reference values in €ct per vkm.*

Table 3.
Reference and adjusted values of marginal external costs for transport in SEE countries, €ct/tkm.

- Network types are defined by routes and sections as stated in **Table 3** (single or double lane, electrified, or non-electrified), as well as the type of trains, vkm, and tkm for each type and section of the network;
- As the Handbook (2020) recommends the marginal values in €ct/train km or tkm, they are adjusted to 2021, accounting for the current economic conditions by using respective coefficients, which have been already mentioned above;
- The adjusted marginal values are multiplied by the total volumes (vkm or tkm) to calculate the total external costs for the whole routes and different types of trains.

Finally, the calculation of potential markups included in the infrastructure charges as part of internalizing external transport costs could be calculated per km for every pilot route, as suggested in **Table 5**.

Calculating the marginal external costs by type of vehicles, modes of transport, and different pilot routes are used to present the total external marginal costs for each route by cost category. This creates an opportunity for comparing the costs for different routes. However, it should be considered that the value transfer to different EU countries is sensitive to national and local specifications and is only undertaken because no national studies are available. Therefore, the respective results represent rough estimates only.

As the final calculations show, the total marginal external costs for the movement of different types of vehicles are the lowest for the rail routes. Furthermore, the load capacity of the trains is many times higher than road vehicles, thus providing a better performance of rail transport and lower costs for internalization. Considering the calculated total marginal external costs per km and type of vehicle/train, they could be used for the final calculation of markups to be included in railway infrastructure charges and tolls. The results show that the respective markups increase with the load capacity of vehicles and are the highest for heavy goods vehicles. Something more, the higher the vehicle capacity in road transport, the higher the markups.

In conclusion, it should be noted that it is impossible to compare directly respective costs for different pilot routes because the vehicles used for calculations are different for each mode of transport and have different load capacities. However, if traffic data (for example, number of vehicles running on each route) are available, it would be possible to evaluate the total external costs for the usage of each route for a certain period.

The discussed approach provides an opportunity for higher cost recovery, especially in reflecting external transport costs. Where charges reflect infrastructure, congestion, and other external costs, transport services will ensure full cost recovery

Alternative route	Origin–destination	Segment of the route	Country	Distance (km)	Type of infrastructure
Pilot route I	Thessaloniki - Ljublana along Corridor X (rail)	Thessaloniki - Gevgelija	GR, NM	79	Single, non-electrified track
		Gevgelija-Skopje	NM	165.9	Single, electrified track
		Skopje- Tabanovce/ Pcevo	NM/RS	49	Single, electrified track
		Tabanovce/Pecevo-Nis	NM/RS	160	Single electrified track
		Nis-Stalać	RS	62	Double electrified track/ Single electrified track-Dunis-Stalac
		Stalać - Velika Plana	RS	89	Double electrified track
		Velika Plana - Beograd	RS	104	Single, electrified track
		Beograd- Šid granica/Tovarnik	RS	145	Double electrified track
		Šid granica/ Tovarnik – Novska	RS/HR	185	Double electrified track
		Novska- Dugo Selo	HR	84	Single, electrified track
		Dugo Selo - Dobova/	HR	58	Double electrified track
		Dobova/Ljubljana	HR/SL	150	Double electrified track
		TOTAL		**1330.9**	
Pilot route II (alternative to PR I)	Thessaloniki - Ljublana along Corridor X (road)	Thessaloniki - Veles	GR, NM	182	E75
		Veles - Nis	NM/RS	227	E75
		Nis - Belgrade	RS	241	E70
		Belgrade - Zagreb	RS/HR	394	E70
		Zagreb - Ljubljana	HL/SL	145	E70
			TOTAL	**1189**	E70
Pilot route III	Burgas - Pirot along Corridor X (rail)	Burgas - Voliyak, Sofia	BG	422	1. Burgas- Zimnitza -
					Double electrified track;
					2. Zimnitza-Yambol - Single, electrified track
					3. Yambol-Kermen- Double electrified track;
					4. Kermen -Kalitinova - Single, electrified track Kalitinovo-Mihailovo-Double electrified track;
					5. Mihailovo-Skutare - Single, electrified track;
					6. Skutare-Voluyak - Double electrified track

Alternative route	Origin–destination	Segment of the route	Country	Distance (km)	Type of infrastructure
		Voliyak, Sofia – Dragoman fr./ Dimitrovgrad (border BG/RS)	BG/RS	49	Single, electrified track
		Dragoman fr./ Dimitrovgrad (border BG/RS)- Pirot	RS	33	Single, electrified track
		TOTAL		**504**	
Pilot route IV (alternative to PR III)	Burgas - Pirot along Corridor X (road)	Burgas -Sofia	BG	382	Highway
		Sofia – Dimitrovgrad (border BG/SE)	BG/RS	61.1	E80
		Dimitrovgrad- Pirot	RS	27.1	E80
		TOTAL		**470.2**	

Table 4.
Pilot routes characteristics.

and thus help to balance the country's transport system further. Nevertheless, of course, it is a matter of transport policy decision to define the exact level of external costs covered by the infrastructure charges and to provide a reasonable explanation for the rest of these costs to be covered by the society as a whole, not only by the transport users.

4. Socioeconomic effects of the internalization of external costs for transport

4.1 Distribution effects

The aim of the internalization of external costs of transport in infrastructure charges is to increase the efficiency of transport activity and to provide proper pricing signals to the users for the actual social costs they impose by their modal choices. A compensatory mechanism should be proposed to ensure fair pricing and competition in the transport market if the internalization leads to increased infrastructure charges and undesirable allocation effects. The volume of transport, in general, is increasing, meaning wealthier households spend most of their income on transport. Therefore, determining transport charges based on the proposed approach to internalizing the external costs may have a positive rather than a negative effect on allocation. However, the final effect will depend to a large extent on the increase in costs in the respective mode of transport and on the type of compensation mechanism applied by the state. Thus, the real disposable income will increase for each socioeconomic group.

The implementation of the approach to setting infrastructure charges based on marginal social costs will provide a significant benefit to the whole society, as well. It will lead directly to improved technological, operational, and organizational

Pilot route I – Rail							
Cost category	**Marginal external costs per 2021 per gross weight of train (€)**						
	< = 400 t	**400–600 t**	**600–800 t**	**800–1000 t**	**1000–1200 t**	**1200–1400 t**	**1400–1600 t**
Accidents*	7,06	7,06	7,06	7,06	7,06	7,06	7,06
Congestion	0,00	0,00	0,00	0,00	0,00	0,00	0,00
Air pollution	8,92	13,37	17,83	22,29	26,75	31,20	35,66
Noise***	22,29	33,43	44,58	55,72	66,86	78,01	89,15
Climate change	15,25	22,88	30,51	38,14	45,76	53,39	61,02
Cost of habitat damage	670,82	1006,24	1341,65	1677,06	2012,47	1798,23	2683,30
Well-to-tank emissions	306,5	459,7	612,9	766,1	919,4	820,7	1225,8
Total external costs for the pilot route	**1030,80**	**1542,67**	**2054,54**	**2566,41**	**3078,28**	**2788,57**	**4102,02**
Total external costs per km per train	**0,78**	**1,16**	**1,54**	**1,93**	**2,31**	**2,10**	**3,08**
Pilot route II – Road (alternative to PR I)							
Cost category	**Marginal external costs per 2021 per type of vehicle (€)**						
	<=3.5 t	**3.5–7.5 t**	**7.5–12 t**	**12–20 t**	**20–26 t**	**26–40 t**	**44–60 t**
Accidents	1,92	2,43	2,43	2,43	0,46	0,46	0,46
Congestion**	70,39	532,55	2982,29	4970,48	9066,79	13,948,91	20,923,36
Air pollution***	55,46	30,08	48,13	64,17	83,42	128,34	192,51
Noise****	0,23	0,49	0,79	1,31	1,71	2,63	3,94
Climate change***	52,70	40,18	182,25	243,00	94,36	145,17	217,75
Cost of habitat damage	34,12	13,39	21,43	28,58	37,15	57,15	85,73
Well-to-tank emissions	2,5	4,9	7,9	10,5	13,7	21,0	31,6
Total external costs for the pilot route	**217,34**	**624,06**	**3245,21**	**5320,49**	**9297,56**	**14,303,70**	**21,455,31**
Total external costs per km per vehicle	**0,18**	**0,53**	**2,73**	**4,48**	**7,83**	**12,04**	**18,06**
Pilot route III – Rail							
Cost category	**Marginal external costs per 2021 per gross weight of train (€)**						
	< = 400 t	**400–600 t**	**600–800 t**	**800–1000 t**	**1000–1200 t**	**1200–1400 t**	**1400–1600 t**
Accidents	2,90	2,90	2,90	2,90	2,90	2,90	2,90
Congestion	0,00	0,00	0,00	0,00	0,00	0,00	0,00
Air pollution	3,44	5,16	6,87	8,59	10,31	12,03	13,75
Noise****	10,74	16,11	21,48	26,85	32,22	37,60	42,97
Climate change	0,00	0,00	0,00	0,00	0,00	0,00	0,00
Cost of habitat damage	154,83	187,41	199,90	249,88	299,86	349,83	399,81
Well-to-tank emissions	70,96	106,44	113,54	141,93	170,31	198,70	315,87

Pilot route I – Rail							
Cost category	**Marginal external costs per 2021 per gross weight of train (€)**						
	< = 400 t	**400–600 t**	**600–800 t**	**800–1000 t**	**1000–1200 t**	**1200–1400 t**	**1400–1600 t**
Total external costs for the pilot route	**242,87**	**318,02**	**344,70**	**430,15**	**515,60**	**601,06**	**775,30**
Total external costs per km per train	**0,48**	**0,63**	**0,68**	**0,85**	**1,02**	**1,19**	**1,54**
Pilot route IV – Road (alternative to pilot route III)							
Cost category	**Marginal external costs per 2021 per type of vehicle (€)**						
	<=3.5 t	**3.5–7.5 t**	**7.5–12 t**	**12–20 t**	**20–26 t**	**26–40 t**	**44–60 t**
Accidents	1,11	0,71	0,71	0,71	0,14	0,14	0,14
Congestion**	27,09	203,21	325,14	541,90	4324,66	6653,33	9979,99
Air pollution***	7,90	11,48	18,36	24,49	31,83	48,97	73,46
Noise****	0,09	0,19	0,30	0,51	0,66	1,01	1,52
Climate change***	9,75	43,46	69,54	92,73	36,01	55,39	83,09
Cost of habitat damage	11,85	25,40	40,64	54,19	70,45	108,38	162,57
Well-to-tank emissions	0,88	1,88	3,01	4,01	5,22	8,03	12,04
Total external costs for the pilot route	**58,67**	**286,34**	**457,72**	**718,53**	**4468,96**	**6875,25**	**10,312,81**
Total external costs per km per vehicle	**0,12**	**0,61**	**0,97**	**1,53**	**9,50**	**14,62**	**21,93**

*Notes: * The marginal accident costs are calculated based on the reference values in €ct/vehicle km.*
Values for 3,5 t vehicle are for morning peak (max).Values for 3.5 t vehicles are for gasoline.****Values for 3,5 t vehicle and 400 t train are for the day and dense traffic.*

Table 5.
Total marginal external costs by cost category and pilot routes.

efficiency, the necessary minimum changes in the modal shift, and a minimal reduction in demand for transport.

4.2 Effects in the field of integration of underdeveloped areas

Implementing the infrastructure charging system, in line with the proposed approach, will also change transport prices in peripheral or underdeveloped areas. The charges will be differentiated to have a lower impact on areas with less congestion and pollution. Therefore, charges reflecting the related costs in rural and peripheral areas where infrastructure is low and there is no congestion will be lower. Furthermore, as highlighted above, the system is likely to generate significant benefits that can be targeted at less developed areas. In case higher infrastructure charges hamper the economic development of peripheral and underdeveloped areas, the reform of the infrastructure charging system must be implemented flexibly and smoothly, providing that it does not distort competition. Difficulties will arise when the infrastructure facilities concerned are the only links with the rest of the country or are important business centers for the local economy. On the other hand, where transport infrastructure capacity is relatively low, significant investments are needed to increase accessibility to accommodate increased traffic. Therefore, there may be a need to apply charges leading to higher cost recovery.

Differentiated infrastructure charges will cause changes in the structure and distribution of transport costs. They will reduce transport costs for the whole society and reduce direct costs for some producers. Moreover, transport costs will increase for producers who cannot change their behavior per these charges. As already stated, transport costs have a relatively low share in the total production costs of industrial enterprises. In the short term, some producers will be partially affected if they are located in peripheral areas, dependent on the only mode of transport, and selling their products in small markets in competition with other domestic producers. Local authorities in these peripheral areas may take measures to support the competitiveness of the producers concerned in the central markets. They may assist them in adapting the product structure to support products of higher value and with a higher relative share and by improving the quality of the main transport links.

4.3 Economic effects

From a general economic point of view, the long-term effect of external costs' internalization will have little and no indirect impact on GDP growth but will allow for secondary benefits through revenue growth. Improving the infrastructure charging system will provide a more accurate basis for comparing returns on investment in transport and improving conditions for private investment and infrastructure operation. When introducing direct infrastructure charges, each shipment can be assessed according to the costs and benefits incurred, as all costs will be considered. This will create opportunities for transport services to deliver economic profit. On the other hand, internalizing the environmental costs will increase environmental efficiency and sustainability, i.e., where the charges reflect the costs of removing harmful emissions, the level of such emissions will fall to the point where the costs of reducing them will equalize the benefits of this measure. In this way, in terms of social efficiency, the well-being of society will be maximized, not the number of trips.

From a financial point of view, more efficient use of the transport system will reduce the need for government spending on infrastructure, health, and environmental protection. The net effect in the commercial sector will be positive. The direct effect of higher transport charges will be offset by reducing congestion and accident costs and any possible tax reductions provided by the government. There may be some decrease in transport-intensive industries where transport costs are high at the final cost of production. However, this decrease will be slight as the overall increase in transport prices will be slow, and companies will regulate (adjust) their material and technical supply and production.

For each transport mode, the relative price changes will vary depending on the cost structure as well as the initial structure of the infrastructure charging system. Nevertheless, the primary data from the various studies in the EU concerning the impact of changes in transport charges show that the net well-being of consumers is improving. Furthermore, these results show that the benefits achieved by reducing congestion and pollution and reducing tax payments outweigh the losses arising from the price increases of the transport services concerned.

Urban transport surveys show that price changes are causing positive technological changes, with peak hour traffic in cities reduced by 19–33% and external costs reduced by 13–35%. In public transport, the use of private vehicles has decreased, while the volume of public passenger transport has increased. The number of road accidents was reduced by 20%, and the average waiting time during peak periods was reduced by 16%. Therefore, introducing the approach based on internalizing external costs can lead to an overall positive outcome in society's well-being [21]. By returning fee revenues to the economy through reductions in income taxes, production, employment, and economic growth will be stimulated. All these effects will outweigh the impact of increased transport prices.

Establishing an infrastructure accounting system in transport must focus on allocating responsibilities between different levels of state governance (local, regional, infrastructure managers, country). In order to assess the actual infrastructure costs properly, it is necessary to focus the efforts on coordination between the different transport and infrastructure operators and the institutions concerned to improve information security and statistics. In this context, it is imperative to implement appropriate and applicable policy rules and actions to provide cost data and other economic and social information for the transport sector. The measures of such a policy must be aimed at drawing up guidelines and proposals for legislation on the setting of transport infrastructure charges.

Appropriate actions in this direction are as follows:

- Development of methodologies for assessing the external cost of transport infrastructure by mode of transport;
- Support of transport accounting at the national level;
- Development of accounting practices to ensure the cost calculation;
- Specifying the needs for statistics and surveys, defining priorities, and reviewing the practice of setting charges.
- Conduct studies on assessing infrastructure costs, measurement, and principles applied in transport accounting to define the necessary level of recovery for infrastructure costs.

5. Conclusions

The discussed approach to improving the infrastructure charging system in transport by internalizing external costs guarantees the effectiveness and linking of charges for the use of transport infrastructure with the relevant costs in all transport modes. Its implementation will increase the efficiency of the transport industry as a whole. Changing the charges by applying this approach will impact the level of infrastructure usage and lead to a higher level of cost recovery directly from users. Furthermore, the aim is not to increase or decrease charges for certain modes of transport but to justify the size of the different elements in setting them and the need for state subsidies [26]. Thus, better communication between transport infrastructure market participants will be achieved, and the actions and interests of each of them will be synchronized. This measure will create an opportunity to achieve the objectives related to improving transport infrastructure usage and sustainable development of the transport systems. In addition, significant economic and social effects will be achieved at the national level.

It is also necessary to improve existing infrastructure, ensure a shift to environmentally friendly modes of transport and use economic instruments to reduce fuel consumption, greenhouse gas emissions, and noise. The main objective of this is to increase the efficiency and sustainability of the countries' transport systems and to stimulate the competitiveness of the national economies.

The discussed approach is based on the following basic principles:

- developing standard basic requirements for the setting of infrastructure charges based on markups for external costs in different modes of transport;

- infrastructure charges must be based on the "user pays" principle, according to which all users of transport infrastructure pay the costs they cause;

- the level and nature of the use of the infrastructure must have a direct link to the costs and other effects (social or environmental) caused by the users;

- in order to reduce distortions of competition, different charges may be applied for the use of the same type of transport infrastructure only where there are significant differences in infrastructure costs and no discrimination is allowed for specific users;

- the infrastructure charging system in transport must ensure high efficiency in the development and use of infrastructure and ensure a public and environmentally acceptable level of usage.

The internalization of external infrastructure costs applies to all modes of transport. However, the costs' content and values vary depending on the transport mode and the conditions for access to the infrastructure (e.g., time of day and place). Cost analysis by type of transport infrastructure shows insufficient information assurance concerning part of the marginal, respectively, variable costs. This fact means that it is impossible to accurately assess all marginal costs (internal and external), and acceptable approximations are required to establish a relatively objective basis for allocating costs and charges. The non-reflectance of external costs in infrastructure charges currently leads to a significant distortion and rebalancing of intermodal competition. On the other hand, this is also the reason for the application of charges, which reduce the efficiency of transport infrastructure and send wrong price signals to transport users.

Sponsorship

The research presented in the chapter is funded by an academic project № INI – KP-06-DK2/4 of 30.03.2021 supported by the Bulgarian National Science Fund of the Ministry of Education and Science.

Author details

Christina Nikolova
University of National and World Economy, Sofia, Bulgaria

*Address all correspondence to: hrnikolova@unwe.bg

IntechOpen

© 2022 The Author(s). Licensee IntechOpen. This chapter is distributed under the terms of the Creative Commons Attribution License (http://creativecommons.org/licenses/by/3.0), which permits unrestricted use, distribution, and reproduction in any medium, provided the original work is properly cited.

References

[1] OECD. External Costs of Transport in Central and Eastern Europe. Vienna: OECD Environment Directorate; 2010

[2] Essen H et al. Handbook on the External Costs of Transport: Version 2019 – 1.1. Directorate-General for Mobility and Transport, European Commission. Brussels: Publications Office; 2020. DOI: 10.2832/51388

[3] Wijngaarden L et al. Sustainable Transport Infrastructure Charging and Internalization of Transport Externalities: Executive Summary. Directorate-General for Mobility and Transport, European Commission. Brussels: European Commission; 2019. DOI: 10.2832/246834

[4] Monden R, El Beyrouty K, Gatto M, et al. Overview of Transport Infrastructure Expenditures and Costs. Directorate-General for Mobility and Transport, European Commission. Brussels: Publications Office; 2019. DOI: 10.2832/853267

[5] European Commission. White Paper: Fair Payment for Infrastructure Use: A Phased Approach to a Common Transport Infrastructure Charging Framework in the EU. Brussels: European Commission; 1998

[6] Beyrouty K et al. Transport Taxes and Charges in Europe: An Overview Study of Economic Internalization Measures Applied in Europe. Directorate-General for Mobility and Transport, European Commission. Brussels: Publications Office; 2019. DOI: 10.2832/416737

[7] LIBERAIL. Methodology for Determination of the Costs of Using the Infrastructure, Work Package 3. Brussels: LIBERAIL; 2001

[8] Doll C, Jansson J. User costs and benefits. In: Matthews B, Nash C, editors. Measuring the Marginal Social Costs of Transport. Amsterdam, Oxford: Elsevier; 2005

[9] Bickel P et al. Deliverable 11: Environmental Marginal Cost Case Studies. Leeds: UNITE: Institute for Transport Studies, University of Leeds; 2003

[10] Preiss P, Friedrich R, Klotz V. New Energy Externalities Development for Sustainability (NEEDS). Stuttgart: University of Stuttgart; 2008

[11] ITT. WP 6: ADB and Green Transport, Deliverable 6.1 External Costs of Transport in ADB Area: Lessons Learnt. Ljubljana: Institute of Traffic and Transport; 2013

[12] Proost S, Van Dender K. Marginal social cost pricing for all transport modes and the effects of modal budget constraints. Working Paper Series. 2003; **11**:1-34

[13] Quinet E, Vickerman R. Principles of Transport Economics. Cheltenham: Edward Elgar; 2004. pp. 134-146

[14] Bickel P. Environmental marginal cost case studies. In: Matthews B, Nash C, editors. Unification of Accounts and Marginal Costs for Transport Efficiency. Leeds: University of Leeds; 2003

[15] High-Level Group on Infrastructure Charging. Calculating Transport Environmental Costs. Brussels: Final Report of the Expert Advisors to the High-Level Group on Infrastructure Charging; 1999

[16] High-Level Group on Infrastructure Charging. Calculating Transport

Accident Costs. Working Group 3, Final Report of the Expert Advisors to the High-Level Group on Infrastructure Charging, 27 April 1999. Brussels: European Commission. p. 1999

[17] High-Level Group on Infrastructure Charging. Calculating Transport Infrastructure Costs. Working Group 1, Final Report of the Expert Advisors to the High-Level Group on Infrastructure Charging, 28 April 1999. Brussels: European Commission. p. 1999

[18] Miola A et al. Review of the Measurement of External Costs of Transportation in Theory and Practice. Maritime Transport. Report 1. Institute for Environment and Sustainability, Joint Research Centre. Brussels: Publications Office; 2011

[19] Brooks L, Liscow Z. Infrastructure costs. Washington: American Economic Journal: Applied. 2019:1-76. DOI: 10.2139/ssrn.3428675

[20] High-Level Group on Transport Infrastructure Charging. Final Report on Estimating Transport Costs, 26 May 1999. Brussels: European Commission; 1999

[21] Becker U, Becker T, Gerlach J. The True Costs of Automobility: External Costs of Cars - Overview on Existing Estimates in EU-27. Dresden: Technical University of Dresden; 2012

[22] Link H, Herry M, et al. Deliverable 10: Case studies on marginal infrastructure costs. In: Unification of Accounts and Marginal Costs for Transport Efficiency. Leeds: University of Leeds; 2002. p. 5

[23] Bossche M et al. Marginal cost methodology. In: Unification of Accounts and Marginal Costs for Transport Efficiency. Leeds: University of Leeds; 2002

[24] Johansson P, Nilsson J. An Economic Analysis of Track Maintenance Costs. Deliverable 10: Annex A3. Unification of Accounts and Marginal Costs for Transport Efficiency. Leeds: University of Leeds; 2002. p. 6

[25] Nikolova C. Evaluating average external costs of inland freight transport in south-eastern European countries: Policy implications, economic. Alternatives Journal. 2015;**3**:64-81

[26] Institute of Traffic and Transport Ljubljana. WP 6: ADB and Green Transport, Deliverable 6.1 External Costs of Transport in ADB Area: Lessons Learnt. Ljubljana: Institute of Traffic and Transport; 2013. pp. 218-240

Chapter 6

Perspective Chapter: Roadmap to a Holistic Highway Digital Twin – A Why, How, and Why Framework

Ashtarout Ammar, Hala Nassereddine and Gabriel Dadi

Abstract

The advent and spread of the COVID-19 pandemic shifted the world's focus toward investing in social structure projects that would improve urbanization and enhance equity. This shift compiled with the emergence of innovative technologies namely Digital Twins, allowed for investigating new approaches for designing and delivering infrastructures, thus paving the road toward smarter infrastructures. Smart infrastructures achieved by connecting the physical aspect of the infrastructure with its digital aspect will allow for optimizing the performance of infrastructure systems by digitally enhancing the asset value and leveraging the value of asset data. Digital Twins can be applied to several civil infrastructure projects including the transportation sector. Also, Digital Twins can be implemented for different spatial scales, on a national level, on the level of the city, and for a network of assets. Few case studies described how to transfer a Digital Twin vision to practice; thus, this chapter presents the journey for a holistic Digital Twin for a highway system formed of a network of assets by discussing the Why, How, and What framework. A holistic highway Digital Twin will allow for cross-asset data analysis, conducting predictive and preventive maintenance, and efficient resource allocation based on data-driven decision-making.

Keywords: digital Twins, data management, data management system, civil infrastructure systems, highway system, transportation assets

1. Introduction

In 2019, the world witnessed a global crisis caused by the emergence and spread of COVID-19 an infectious disease that caused the death of millions of people [1]. With the emergence of the pandemic, it was evident that the lack of focus on sustainable development goals (SDGs), especially the ones related to people and the environment, played an important role in the emergence and spread of infectious diseases, including COVID-19 [2]. The resulting chaos caused by the pandemic urged a shift in goals and investments toward health and infrastructure [3]. Thus, the pandemic has accelerated the shift toward social infrastructure projects targeting urbanization, healthcare, infrastructure, and Global Water, Sanitation, & Hygiene (WASH) projects, which will help cities to face future pandemics [4, 5]. This shift motivated governments to upgrade systems to achieve a more resilient and sustainable infrastructure ecosystem

IntechOpen

and consider implementing and adopting technologies within the architectural, engineering, construction, and operation (AECO) industry [6, 7].

Some governments started this shift before the pandemic to help overcome the challenges of the AECO industry and improve the industry's digitization capability. For instance, the United Kingdom (UK) in their 2018 construction sector deal, a partnership between the government and the construction sector, dedicated £600 billion of investment in infrastructure including £31billion to boost digital construction and smart infrastructure [8]. Conversely, in the United States (US), in November 2021, the Infrastructure Investment and Jobs Act (IIJA) was officially legislated. The IIJA is a $1.2 trillion investment, representing the "largest investment in the nation's critical infrastructure systems in a generation or more" [9]. The new law will allow for the investment of $110 billion in funding for roads, bridges, and major infrastructure projects. This investment will support mitigating the impact of climate change, building resilient and sustainable infrastructure, enhancing equity, and improving safety for road users of all modes [10]. Moreover, the law dedicated $100 million to fund the digital construction management systems and related technologies program. It is anticipated that this program will support the investment in technologies and tools including visual-based inspection technologies, construction management tools, electronic ticketing (e-ticketing), Digital Twins, and unmanned aerial vehicles (UAVs) [11].

Smart infrastructure—or the combination of the physical aspect of the infrastructure with its digital aspect—is a global opportunity worth £2 trillion to £4.8 trillion [12]. Smart infrastructures will allow for a better understanding of the performance of the existing infrastructure system, thus optimizing its efficiency and supporting the design and delivery of new infrastructure systems [12]. The concept of connecting the physical aspect of assets with its digital model aligns with the concept of Digital Twins, which was defined by several researchers as the digital representation of physical assets, or a digital model created to depict either an existing, ongoing, or future construction project and linked throughout its lifecycle [13, 14]. The authors of [14] highlighted the notion of the Digital Twins for the construction project lifecycle and emphasized the different capabilities of the technology including increased transparency of information, real-time monitoring, analysis, and feedback, better stakeholder collaboration, advanced preventive measures, advanced what-if scenario analysis and simulation, real-time tracking, and higher accuracy.

The concept of Digital Twins emerged with the Fourth Industrial Revolution, known as Construction 4.0 in the AECO industry. However, among the technologies under the umbrella of Construction 4.0, Digital Twins is the least researched in the industry [15] and, while its definitions and applications vary from one sector to the other, its framework is similar [12]. For smart infrastructures, the framework of Digital Twins can be presented as a pyramid formed of a base and three layers. The base is formed of raw data collected using several tools and methods including customer billing, sensors, drone surveys, laser surveys, building information modeling (BIM), geographic information system (GIS), and control systems, among others. On top of the base, resides the data management layer such as data storage, data cleaning, data structure, and other practices related to data management. The layer above data management is data analysis and interpretation or making sense of the existing data. Finally, the crown of the pyramid (i.e., the third layer) is decision-making. As such, to leverage the process of data-driven decision-making, it is essential to lower the data volume (i.e., layer 1) and increase the data value (i.e., layer 3) where the three layers are internally and externally connected by communicating information as presented in **Figure 1** [12].

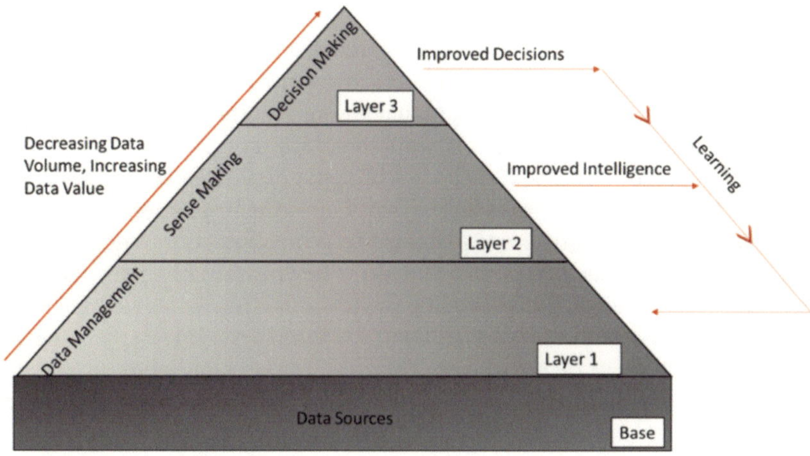

Figure 1.
Digital Twins model for smart infrastructure (adopted from [12]).

This chapter thoroughly investigates the existing research on Digital Twins in the infrastructure industry (Section 2), the applications of Digital Twins in the transportation sector (i.e., bridges, rails, tunnels, and highways) (Section 3), and the implementation of Digital Twins for different spatial scales in the civil infrastructure industry (i.e., national level, city level, and for a network of assets) (Section 4). Additionally, this chapter discusses the vision for a holistic Digital Twin for a highway system (Section 5) and summarizes major findings in a conclusion section (Section 6).

2. Existing research on Digital Twins in the infrastructure industry

Digital Twins originated in aerospace engineering; however, with the advancement in technology, the concept is no longer limited to complex systems and can be implemented to provide a digital representation of any system [16]. This feasibility encouraged several researchers from different industries to investigate the concept of Digital Twins. The increased focus on data and the opportunities created by digitization promoted the potential of the emerging phenomenon of Digital Twins in the manufacturing industry with the wave of Industry 4.0 to fulfill the requirements of smart factory [17–19]. The concept of Digital Twins then found its way to the oil and gas industry to optimize offshore operations, reduce risks to health, safety, and environment, and facilitate complex integrated processes [20]. Similarly, the construction industry began considering Digital Twins a key enabler for its digital transformation that could improve the industry's poor record in digitization [14, 21]. Moreover, the digital transformation of engineering assets increased the interest of both researchers and practitioners to investigate the implementation of the concept of Digital Twins in the civil infrastructure domain [22].

Several researchers investigated the implementation of Digital Twins in the infrastructure sector. The authors of [23] examined the current practices of implementing Digital Twins through a series of semi-structured interviews with experts and executives from the UK infrastructure industry. Their study found that the current implementations are still not mature and most of them are under development. These implementations included 3D modeling of physical assets, integration of real-time weather forecasts, asset data and information projects, integration of different information systems coming from several organizations (in the construction phase), and contract management systems throughout the supply chain (in the construction phase), procurement of a network management system and its integration with existing systems, sensor data collection, implementation of common data environments, and modeling of systems and control philosophies. Similarly, the authors of [24] conducted a comprehensive review to investigate the implementation of Digital Twins within the civil infrastructure systems (i.e., transportation, energy telecommunication, water and waste, and smart cities). They thoroughly investigated the existing literature, in addition to surveying professionals and interviewing stakeholders. It was also found that the concept of Digital Twins in the infrastructure industry is still in the early stages of development. The authors also highlighted that the major adoption of Digital Twins within the civil infrastructure system was to optimize operations. Also, they emphasized that it is critical to investigate how Digital Twins can be retrofitted into existing infrastructure systems to improve the efficiency of their operation and maintenance. More recently, the authors of [22] conducted a systematic literature review to map the applications of Digital Twins within the road and rail system, telecommunication, and electricity networks. This study showed that the available studies are scarce and that the use of Digital Twins is mainly perceived for the operation and maintenance phase. It was also noted that while Digital Twins can leverage the value of asset information and, thus, improve the process of data-driven asset management decisions, the impact of Digital Twins on the development of asset management programs within infrastructure organizations should be addressed. Since the focus of this chapter is on transportation systems, a comprehensive review of the existing studies on the application of Digital Twins for transportation systems is discussed in the following section.

3. Digital Twins applications for the transportation system

The transportation system includes the sectors of bridges, railroads, tunnels, and highways. Transportation systems are critical for the development of any jurisdiction, they represent the arteries necessary for connecting people, delivering goods, and providing services for economic development. The failure of these systems can result in considerable economic losses [25]. To mitigate the risks of failure and to improve the management of such a critical and aging system, the transportation sector followed suit and investigated the implementation of Digital Twins with a wide variety of applications.

3.1 Digital Twin applications for bridges

Bridges are complex engineering systems and are considered high-value assets with a relatively extended life span; thus, their continuous maintenance to prevent their deterioration and mitigate the risks of their failure is always a priority for infrastructure organizations. As such, the ability to conduct preventive maintenance and lifecycle monitoring of bridges became an essential strategy in the bridge industry since it can support proactive measures to maintain the structural integrity of bridges throughout their entire lifecycle. The capability of Digital Twins to aggregate real-time data and historical data, support data analysis, and enable insights on preventive maintenance captured the attention of researchers in the bridge industry to investigate the potential of implementing Digital Twins in their bridge design, construction, operation and maintenance, and deterioration [26, 27].

A Digital Twin solution to enhance bridge maintenance by integrating a maintenance information management system based on a 3D information model with a digital inspection system using image processing was proposed by the authors of [26]. The proposed model was validated for maintaining pre-stressed concrete bridges where it facilitated the detection of surface damages in a real-time manner, thus providing early warnings of any potential distress and enabling early remedial interventions. Additionally, a closed lifecycle fatigue management driven by Digital Twins for steel bridges was developed by the authors of [27]. The authors discussed the implementation mechanism of Digital Twins in the bridge design phase, the bridge construction phase, the bridge service and operation phase, and the bridge retirement phase. The authors noted that a Digital Twin-driven fatigue management system can support the integration of a diversity of fatigue data including historical fatigue information after the bridge retirement thus providing better insights for the design and management of new bridges.

3.2 Digital Twin applications for railroads

The railway system is no less important than bridges, which is also a complicated system made of several subsystems, where their maintenance and condition monitoring is critical to mitigate the risks and ensuring safety. Asset managers should have access to continuous information related to the railroad conditions to allow for the early detection of any surface abnormalities caused by temperature change, degradation, or component failure and to have the ability to automate and modify railway turnouts or railway switches automatically, in case of an emergency. In that manner, Digital Twins with its capability of integrating multi-sourced data such as data collected by sensors depicting the railroad conditions and weather conditions allows it to act as a centralized data source that can act as a traffic management and control system [28, 29]. The authors of [28] applied the concept of Digital Twins to monitor railway turnouts, a very complicated system by nature of design and construction. Sensors were used to measure the rail temperature promptly and cyclically to support the data acquisition of rail turnouts and to capture emergency conditions. This automated and continuous analysis of the rail components increased the efficiency of managing and maintaining railroad turnouts. Moreover, the concept of Digital Twins for the European Train Control System (ETCS) applications was investigated [29]. The Digital Twin served as a repository and universal simulation environment to support the automatic check and compliance of organizational and operational requirements, system requirement specifications, design principles, regulations governing railway operations, interfaces with the control-command basic layer system, and requirements for the verification process of the control-command subsystem. This resulted in a significant reduction in the duration and cost of validating the ETCS applications.

3.3 Digital Twin applications for tunnels

The development of smart cities and the advancement of available technologies enhanced the utilization of urban underground spaces to construct urban infrastructures such as tunnels. Tunnels are complicated spatial structures and have multiple electromechanical components, such as ventilation systems, necessary for their operation. Digital Twins can support the operation and maintenance of tunnels and allow for lifecycle management analysis [30, 31]. A Digital Twins prototype of noise barrier tunnels (NBTs) was implemented to predict the life and condition of the tunnel components using numerical behavior analysis. Sensors were used to link the behavior of the physical model of the NBT (i.e., a digital model created using a 3D printer) and the digital model of NBT (i.e., a shape-generation script comprised the NBT shape-generation, component-shape generation, and component mapping and layout models) [30]. The implemented Digital Twins prototype allowed for the lifecycle management analysis, which can help reduce NBT installation costs, support the use of recycled materials, and make the process of installation more sustainable by identifying components that should be replaced at the early stages of the NBT design. Moreover, the authors of [31] proposed a Digital Twins-based decision analysis framework for the operation and maintenance of tunnels. The proposed framework defined the decision analysis and an extended Construction-Operations Building information exchange COBie standard-based organization method employed to define information for assets that are delivered as part of facility construction projects and used to document the data with BIM—and integrating data using semantic web technologies. The proposed framework was validated by operating and maintaining complex electromechanical systems such as fans that are used to eliminate harmful gases and control visibility inside the tunnel. The Digital Twin framework supported the early detection of any anomalies in the operation of fans and determining the fault causes. This allowed for taking timely maintenance interventions to ensure better operation of the tunnel.

3.4 Digital Twin applications for highways

Highways are less complicated when compared to other transportation systems in terms of their structure, nevertheless due to their expansion over a vast network and the use of vast quantities of materials their lifecycle management and material durability are always a concern. Multi-sourced data integration enabled by Digital Twins facilitates the prediction of highway materials performance, allows better visualization of key performance indicators (KPIs), and supports reliable and data-driven decision-making [32, 33]. A framework combining Digital Twins and multiple time series stacking (MTSS) was employed to predict the performance of highway tunnel pavement performance [32]. The Digital Twins is formed of three key components: (1) data collection module including pavement performance data collected by performance indicators such as sensors and high precision accelerometers, main maintenance records extracted from the operation and maintenance system, tunnel highway structure, traffic flow, and tunnel environment; (2) prediction model, where a pavement performance prediction model was developed based on multiple differentiated models generated to predict the future performance of selected pavement section; and (3) parametric analysis model, established in the dynamo environment to integrate the multisource spatial-temporal data of the BIM model and the physical assets. The proposed framework was validated using a case study, and it was found that the visuals provided by Digital Twins allowed for conducting preventive maintenance. Similarly, the authors of [33] established a fully functioning Digital Twin of a road constructed using secondary raw materials (SRMs). The model included structured geometric and attribute data related to SRMs such as material data, chemical and mineralogical composition, strength, and unstructured data including real-time material characteristics collected by sensors. The developed Digital Twins supported data centralization and allowed the graphical presentation of KPIs.

3.5 Section summary

Infrastructure projects are complicated construction projects with a lifespan that might expand for a couple of decades. It is well known in the construction industry that the cost of operation and maintenance can be up to two or three times the cost of the initial construction and that it can equate from 60 to 80% of the total lifecycle cost, with the extended lifecycle of infrastructure projects this cost can be significant [34]. Infrastructure asset management constitutes several processes that are data-intensive and necessitates continuous data collection and analysis to support decision-making. The emergence of Construction 4.0 technologies, mainly Digital Twins, facilitated by the availability of powerful and cheaper sensors and cyber-physical systems (CPS) and with the aid of computational technologies such as big data analytics, semantic web-based technologies, and the Internet of Things (IoT) coupled with the drive toward digitizing infrastructure assets and transforming them into "smart infrastructures" provided a more holistic and innovative approach for managing infrastructure assets and informing decision-making.

The use of Digital Twins for transportation systems was mainly implemented to help asset managers better operate and maintain complex and interconnected sub-systems, monitor the performance of different system components, enhance the visualization of information necessary to conduct preventive maintenance and detection of abnormalities, conduct lifecycle management analysis, and take proactive interventions to mitigate failure risks and enhance the system's structural integrity. Moreover, the capability of Digital Twins to act as a centralized hub of meta-data with multiple sources supported the establishment of a universal simulation environment and data repository, thus allowing asset managers to have access to reliable information and therefore allowing them to conduct informed and quality-based decision-makings. However, the discussed studies showed that the implementation of Digital Twins for the transportation system is not mature yet. Most of the studies presented either a practical or conceptual Digital Twins framework that was driven to satisfy its purpose of solving an identified problem. No large-scale Digital Twin for transportation systems was employed where the full potential of Digital Twin is achieved, and their capabilities are optimized. Nevertheless, the proposed frameworks showed promising results toward adopting Digital Twins in the transportation sector.

4. Digital Twins for different spatial scales in the civil infrastructure industry

Sections 2 and 3 showed that Digital Twins can be used for many purposes. It can be used for potential future planning by running what-if simulations, and predictive and preventive maintenance management. Also, it can be implemented in the project's current state for operation and maintenance, real-time monitoring and control, and early detection of abnormalities to optimize the performance of assets. Moreover, it can act as an archive for historical data and provide key insights from past lessons. However, Digital Twins can be used for multiple purposes and can be employed for different spatial scales, that is, on the level of an asset, for a network of assets, for a system or city, and at a national level. As was mentioned in the previous sections, most of the applications of Digital Twins were for a specific purpose and on a small scale and this could pertain to the fact that the concept of Digital Twins in the civil infrastructure industry is not mature yet. Previous studies showed very promising results, and this encouraged several governments, institutions, and organizations to explore the practicality of the concept and build a vision toward optimizing the potential of Digital Twins on a holistic spatial scale and investigate different strategies, frameworks, and roadmaps to bring the vision into action and transform the way of planning, verifying, delivering, and operating the built environment.

4.1 Digital Twins on a national level

The case studies on envisioning the implementation of Digital Twins on a national level are very limited since this is a huge investment and requires the collaboration of several stakeholders. However, the UK is leading in this initiative and the government generated the Industrial Strategy Transforming Construction Programme and established the Center for Digital Built Britain (CDBB) at the University of Cambridge to set definitions and principles across the built environment to develop a roadmap toward a National Digital Twin (NDT); an ecosystem of connected Digital Twins of physical assets to leverage the use of asset data for the benefit of the public [35]. The vision for Digital Built Britain is to "enhance the natural and built environment, thereby driving up commercial competitiveness and productivity as well as quality of life and wellbeing for the public. This will be achieved through better planning, delivery and whole-life management of infrastructure and the wider built environment—enabled by mustering the full power of the information value chain" [13]. It is perceived that the use of an information management framework and an NDT in a coordinated and considered manner will support the release of data from isolated silos and enable the creation of a centralized data repository, resulting in an additional £7 billion/year of benefits across the UK infrastructure sectors [36]. The road map for delivering the information management framework can be addressed by answering the following questions [13]:

1. **Approach**: What is the best overall approach for realizing the benefits of information management across the built environment?

2. **Governance:** What are the best structures and processes for managing the development, adoption, and ongoing oversight of the framework?

3. **Standardization:** What principles, guidance, specifications, and formal standards are required?

4. **Enablers:** What potential blockers are there, and how should they be addressed? What cultural, behavioral, technological, commercial, or other adjustments are necessary?

5. **Change:** What should be done to get the framework adopted across the whole built environment?

To guide the development of the framework and the NDT, CDBB defined the Gemini Principle as the conscience of the framework identified by nine principles and distributed over three clusters (1) purpose, (2) trust, and (3) function [13]. The NDT should have a clear purpose and must be used to provide good to the public, enable value creation and improve performance, and must provide insights into the built environment. Additionally, it should be trustworthy to the public; otherwise it will lose value, data sharing should be open as possible but at the same time should be secured to ensure its integrity and should rely on quality data. Finally, the NDT should function effectively in support of its purpose, must be based on standards with clear data ownership and data governance, and should be flexible to develop and adopt any technological or system evolutions in the future.

4.2 Digital Twins on a city level

Historically, Singapore faced several challenges while planning its built environment to provide a better quality of life to its residents considering that its area is 728.6 km^2 and its urban density is the third worldwide. To face these challenges, the government of Singapore with the aid of several authorities and research foundations developed "Virtual Singapore: A Digital Twin for Planning," a platform providing a dynamic 3D virtual model of the urban areas of Singapore. The government used 2D maps to solve urban challenges; however, with the emergence of 3D models they realized the potential of 3D data in offering planners a more comprehensive platform to design and pilot urban solutions. This innovative program was operated with three strategic objectives, (1) to consolidate research in 3D data, (2) to develop an operational 3D city model and data platform that integrates BIM, 3D GIS, and simulation for planning use by researchers, citizens, and authorities, and (3) develop a 2D/3D Digital Twin for Singapore that offers planners and citizens tools to examine spatial data and test-bed concepts, and observe the impacts of projects in a "Virtual Singapore" before delivery in the real world [37]. The applications of Virtual Singapore include flood risk analysis, the potential for solar panels and green roofs, and monitoring the impact of wind load on vegetation [37].

Similar to Singapore, the city of Vienna has been experiencing continued growth and demand for new buildings, pressuring the city to issue thousands of new building permits every year. The process of building validation and verification is sophisticated and prone to the loss of information between the building authority and the planners and investors. Digitizing this process and using BIM at the early stages of design and being aware of the benefits of Digital Twins will allow building owners to have a Digital Twin model for their facility that they can use throughout the facility lifecycle and will provide authorities with an efficient building verification and a permission process. For that purpose, the city of Vienna worked with TU Wein and experts from different engineering and architectural firms and consultants on a project titled BRISE-Vienna, an openBIM-based building submission process aiming to integrate the building authority into the Digital Twin of a construction project throughout its lifecycle [14]. The development and maintenance of a Digital Twin for all buildings provide the building authority access to up-to-date Digital Twins throughout the phases of the building lifecycle. The sum of the Digital Twins of all buildings results in a Digital Twin of the city, named an Urban Digital Twin (UDT). UDT creates new opportunities for strategic considerations (urban mining, area analysis, and fire protection analysis) and further research activities (data basis for AI training and thermal simulation). Hence, UDT allows the city to perform advanced what-if scenario analysis and simulations to simulate the change of power supply or heating systems in a whole area for instance (i.e., change to district heating) [14].

4.3 Digital Twins for a network of assets

The government in the UK is very ambitious about being the world leader in shaping the future of infrastructure; for that purpose, they set their vision for Digital

Themes	Subthemes	Description
 *Created by Iconstock from Noun project* Digital Design & Construction	Digitally enabled design	Activities will be automated, modular, and conducted off-site, resulting in safer production, reduced disruption, increased productivity, and smoother journeys
	Modular & standardized approaches	
	Automated construction	
 *Created by Aficons from Noun project* Digital Operations	Intelligent Asset Management	Operations will leverage data to drive increasingly pre-emptive interventions - resulting in improved asset resilience, increased asset life, and a safer, smoother-running network
	Enhanced operational capability	
	Digitally enabled workers	
 *Created by Sunardi from Noun project* Digital for Customers	Information Provision	Customers will be better informed and have trust in the journey information they access, ensuring that they feel safe and in control of their journeys.
	Customer engagement	
	Partnerships & alliances	

Table 1.
Core themes for UK Digital Road Vision 2025.

Roads from 2020 to 2025 and are working on the longer vision of 2050. It is perceived that Digital Roads will harness data, technology, and connectivity to enhance the way the strategic road network (SRN) is designed, constructed, operated, and used. This will allow for safer traveling, faster delivery, and an optimized customer experience [38]. The vision toward Digital Roads is built based upon three core themes as presented in **Table 1** [39].

By the same token, several state Departments of Transportation (DOTs) in the US followed suit and investigated how they can embrace Digital Twins to leverage the value of enterprise asset information to conduct daily operations, monitor performance, and provide transparency to the public. For instance, Utah DOT (UDOT) envisioned Digital Twins as an information management strategy to connect enterprise asset information to a geospatial model of individual physical assets. Digital Twins is foreseen to support the documentation of the planned and as-constructed (as-built) updates and therefore to fill the gap in the information across project development for priority assets, thus ensuring the collection of the necessary information to document asset histories and proper governance of the asset current state [40, 41]. Moreover, at the organizational level, the Digital Twins of the transportation asset systems will provide a single source of reliable, real-time information that will be used across different divisions of the department and the public enabling UDOT to perform complex analyses and make holistic decisions to improve safety, enhance mobility, and preserve the transportation infrastructure [41]. Additionally, UDOT identified several tactical goals with a two-year horizon considered high-value activities with no pre-requisites, and strategic goals with a five-year horizon which are also considered high-value activities with pre-requisites and requires further collaboration. The identified tactical and strategic goals required for the achievement of the overarching objective of adopting Digital Twins for infrastructure assets are summarized in **Table 2** [41].

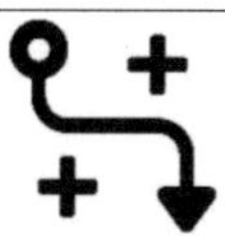 **Tactical goals (2 years horizon)**	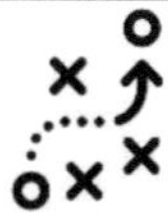 **Strategic goals (5 years horizon)**
Created by Ayub Irawan from Noun project	*Created by Gregor Cresnar from Noun project*
Analyze the business architecture. Find ways to improve how to develop projects,	Use automation to harvest asset information from project data.
Govern project data, define the rules, roles, and responsibilities for data.	Simplify how information is collected to increase consistency and focus on priority activities in construction.
Finalize the model development standards manual and use it on all design projects.	Roll out the policies, tools, and roles for data governance in the development of projects.
Use a repeatable process in construction to update the asset information created in the design.	Use the two prototype Digital Twins on all projects with those assets. Create Digital Twins for other assets.
Build a prototype Digital Twin for two assets (examples, single post signs and barrier). Pilot the Digital Twins on projects.	Make the Digital Twin program sustainable. Invest in Digital Twins to bring value to UDOT as technology changes.
	Adopt the concept of Digital Twin across all groups within the Department.

Table 2.
Tactical and strategic goals identified by the Utah Department of Transportation for a successful implementation of Digital Twins for infrastructure assets.

4.4 Section summary

Envisioning Digital Twins on a large spatial scale is starting to sound appealing among governments, institutions, and organizations. Few envisioned implementing Digital Twins on a national level, others proposed its implementation to face the challenges associated with planning urban environments in developed cities, while some intended to use it for a network of infrastructure assets to digitize the design, construction, and operation of transportation networks or to manage the data of priority assets and fill the gap of the enterprise information.

Each presented vision started by identifying the purpose behind adopting Digital Twins for infrastructures and they established a set of certain principles, themes, strategic objectives, or goals that they considered necessary for achieving the overarching objective of this adoption. Also, they discussed the expected benefits resulting from this implementation. However, there is a lack of pilot projects or actual studies that implemented Digital Twins and explained the transition from vision to action. In the next section, we are going to discuss the vision toward a holistic Digital Twin for a highway system and to further understand how to move from concept to practice, a case study is presented.

5. Journey for a holistic Digital Twin for a highway system—the why, what, and how

A vision for a holistic Digital Twin is initiated by identifying the purpose by answering the *Why* component, or in other words, *Why is a holistic Digital Twin for a*

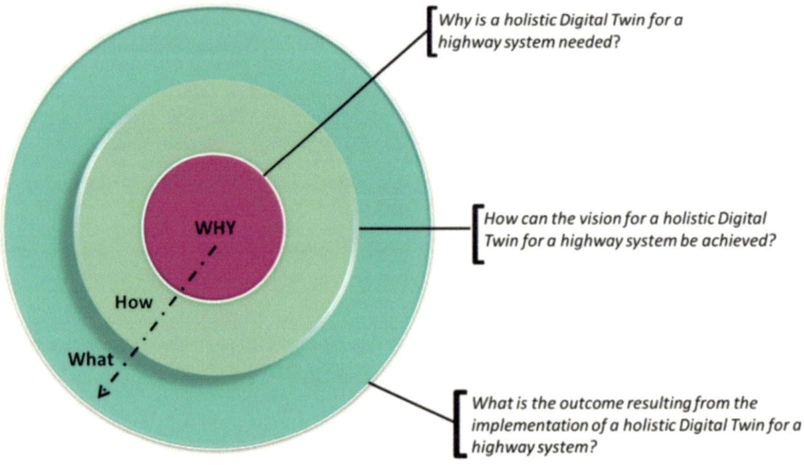

Figure 2.
The why, how, and what components of a holistic Digital Twin for a highway system.

highway system needed? where a clear statement describing the purpose is generated. After declaring the overall purpose, a set of principles, themes, strategies, or goals are formed for setting the *How* component, that is, the process, or in other words, *How can the vision for a holistic Digital Twin for a highway system be achieved?*, which can be described by setting short- and long-term objectives that should be achieved to fulfill the overarching objective for adopting a holistic Digital Twin. Finally, *What* component should be investigated, that is, *What is the outcome resulting from the implementation of a holistic Digital Twin for a highway system?* The Why, How, and What components of a holistic Digital Twin for a highway system are presented in **Figure 2**. In the following sub-sections, the three research questions will be addressed.

5.1 Why the need for a holistic Digital Twin for a highway system

A highway asset system within a state Department of Transportation (DOT) can be classified into three categories: bridges, pavements, and ancillary assets. Usually, state DOTs prioritize the management of high-value assets and highly-visible ones such as pavements and bridges. However, transportation systems extend beyond pavement and bridges to include a wide variety of ancillary assets [42]. Ancillary assets represent a significant investment of public funds and many are essential for the safe and efficient operation of highway facilities including, for instance, access ramps, guardrail end treatments, pavement markings, signs, culverts, drain inlets and outlets, communication systems, and intelligent transportation system (ITS), among others. DOTs are responsible for managing highway assets; thus, they are responsible for collecting, storing, managing, and analyzing vast amounts of asset data to support the process of transportation asset management (TAM) [43]. Every year state DOTs conduct hundreds of projects and make changes to existing ones. New construction projects require the generation of new sets of data to be included in the current database. On the other hand, reconstruction, rehabilitation, asset demolition, or other major maintenance activities require revising and updating the database. All changes conducted for assets through the project execution and its whole lifecycle should be collected accurately and promptly to ensure effective TAM and proper operation and maintenance (O&M) [44]. However, state DOTs are facing several challenges integrating data across systems and throughout the asset lifecycle [45], and they need to focus on six major data management practices that are data collection, data handling, data flow, data transfer, data governance, and data integration to achieve a seamless data management approach and improve the value of data to enable informed decision-making [46].

Conversely, with the emergence of technologies and the notion of data-driven decision-making, where data itself is considered a high-value asset, state DOTs changed their perspective on operational performance where they focused more on operating and maintaining the existing transportation system instead of expanding it, and thus, they are investigating new approaches to manage and operate their transportation assets [47]. However, operating and maintaining existing assets is a sophisticated process and requires complicated decision-making since state DOTs need to identify for each asset a defined management strategy, select priority assets, and make cross-asset resource allocation decisions that would consider multiple objectives [42]. Moreover, transportation asset management requires the existence of spatial metadata with heterogeneous data features coming from multi-sources, in addition to data throughout the asset lifecycle, that is, asset history (e.g., as planned asset data), the current state of the asset (e.g., as-constructed asset data), and real-time data about the asset condition to allow for asset condition monitoring and control. Given the relatively extended life of assets, state DOTs need to use tools and technologies that will enable them to access reliable and informative data to support a lifecycle management approach and adopt data management approaches that can evolve with the evolution of technologies and future data requirements.

Furthermore, asset management can be explained as the task of connecting the fundamental mission of an organization of operating the infrastructure, that is, connecting the digital aspect of the asset and its physical aspect to ensure better asset operation and maintenance and support decision making [48]. This concept of asset management of connecting the physical and digital aspects of assets intersects with the concept of Digital Twins for infrastructure [40]. As such, with the capabilities of Digital Twins in supporting decision-making by providing one source of data registry and a simulation environment to allow for the conduction of prognostic and diagnostic maintenance, in addition to its ability to integrate multi-sourced data and provide enhanced data visualizations, the concept of Digital Twins can be adopted by state DOTs to transform their way of designing, delivering, and operating and maintaining their transportation assets. However, to optimize the use of the concept of Digital Twins, a holistic Digital Twin for the highway system is necessary, since a globalized highway Digital Twin includes informative data about all assets constituting a highway ecosystem and how they interact with each other and with the surrounding environment, thus allowing state DOTs to have better insights toward managing cross-asset systems and make decisions on resource allocation to optimize the performance of cross-asset systems, and the overall highway system.

5.2 How to achieve the vision for a holistic Digital Twin for a highway system

After identifying *Why* is a holistic Digital Twin for a highway system is needed, it is important to understand how the vision can be translated into action. The best way to fulfill this understanding is to learn from leading organizations that succeeded in putting visions into practice. A case study is a form of qualitative research that offers an in-depth examination of the topic [48]. The case study presented in this section started as a vision where the facility management department within the Sydney

Opera House imagined having a 3D model of the facility where they can fly around, select different assets, and view all the related information in one system. This vision was put into practice, where a Digital Twin providing a single source of information for regular building operational requirements and ongoing projects was created.

5.2.1 Digital Twins from vision to action: a facility management case study

The Sydney Opera House was added to UNESCO's World Heritage List in 2007 and is a multi-venue performing art center located at Sydney Harbor in Sydney, New South Wales, Australia. It is one of the country's most iconic and distinctive buildings. The building welcomes more than 8.2 million visitors a year, presenting more than 2000 shows 363 days a year for more than 1.5 million people [49]. The management and maintenance of the building are very challenging because of the special purpose that the building serves and the required technicalities, for instance, when the Sydney Symphony Orchestra is on stage in the concert hall, the room temperature must be maintained at 22.5 degrees to ensure the instruments stay in tune [50]. The building has more than 1000 rooms and managing the use of spaces is dynamic. For instance, spaces might be used for other purposes such as using lifts as dressing rooms for certain shows, partitioning different rooms, or merging spaces to expand the capacity and make use of the added space. The budget for the yearly maintenance of the Sydney Opera House amounts to $30 million AUS (equivalent to £16.5 million or $20.7 million) [51], thus aiming to reduce this high cost, the managers of the Sydney Opera House started investigating innovative solutions to support them in achieving their objective.

As such, in 2013 the BIM Academy (one of the world's leading research and strategic consultants in the global digital built environment established by Northumbria University and Ryder Architecture) won a worldwide tender for the contract to write a detailed BIM strategy to support the facility management (FM) of the Sydney Opera House. Writing the technical piece of the BIM-based facility management required a comprehensive review and thorough investigation of the existing disparate systems that were used to operate the building, methods of documentation, and the current approaches to information modeling. More than 350 interviews with the Sydney Opera House facility managers and employees were conducted to establish a roadmap and write a detailed technical specification for the BIM for FM interface that would connect the facility existing data and future data to the BIM model. The technical specification identified the requirements, developed a model management plan describing the process of developing the 3D models on site, and identified the information that should be included. This phase of the project facilitated the achievement of the second phase which is delivering the Digital Twins platform of the Sydney Opera House.

For the second phase of the project, the BIM Academy collaborated with AECOM (a global multidisciplinary consultancy), and EcoDomus (a leading software developer), to tender and subsequently win the delivery of a Digital Twin-enabled facility management platform for the Sydney Opera House. Alongside that, they won a bid to reformat their documentation system and their spatial management system by expanding their capacity to support the newly developed system. This phase of the project was executed in two stages. The first stage involved recouping and integrating information from the existing database with the newly established database within the 3D model. The second stage introduced a broader range of functional systems that can be added to the BIM interface over time. The aim was to improve the existing Technical Document database (TDOC) and develop a new spatial record management system. The new system encompasses the 3D model and will act as a parent system for all other sub-systems such as the document management system, spatial management system, asset register, and condition management system, and will support the establishment of one source of true data. TDOC will improve efficiency by eliminating wasted efforts and providing usability improvements. Changes such as updating the types of information that could be added to a document, editing information, adding functionalities to edit significant numbers of documents in bulk, and updating the system became more feasible and can be done promptly.

The vision of delivering a Digital Twin platform for the Sydney Opera House was thus achieved over two phases where each phase had several stages. Business analysis was first conducted, followed by comprehensive, structured research and a review of existing information systems and technical and IT infrastructure. Next, integration for systems was designed and innovative potential solutions were solicited. Then, model management was planned and a technical specification with a road map was established. Finally, Digital Twin delivery and implementation were achieved, and user approval, training, and testing were accomplished. The created Digital Twin platform enabled facility managers to have access to reliable geometry and to operate the building easily. Moreover, the platform is not only used by facility managers, but it can also be used by marketing teams to organize events and design and plan seats; security teams to plan logistics around new events; and site management, for instance, removing large bits of equipment and implementing others. The Sydney Opera House implemented the Digital Twin platform as an innovative solution to have better access to asset information, so they can have a diagnostic approach and solve problems promptly. It is expected that the feasible access to information would save on average 30 minutes per work order, for instance, if they have 20,000 work orders per year with an average cost of $50 per hour, they can save up to $500,000 per year. In the future, the Sydney Opera House is envisioning optimizing the use of the Digital Twin platform to support solving any future problems that they might face and keep updating the platform to manage any additional subsystems or any future advancement in data and technologies.

5.2.2 Digital Twins from vision to action: case of a highway system

State DOTs, responsible for managing and maintaining highway assets, have created, collected, and stored transportation asset data; however, the available data structures are not consistent, and they are either unstructured data (e.g., documents), semi-structured (e.g., excel data sheets), or structured data (e.g., databases). State DOTs are trying to improve their digitization capacity by collecting data in digital formats and abandoning the use of papers, improving the quality of collected data, and using automated and remote techniques to collect asset data [40]. However, data exist in isolated silos, with no further understanding of how these data should be integrated and managed. Therefore, to achieve the vision of Digital Twins for a highway system, state DOTs need to put a set of objectives and goals as a roadmap toward a holistic highway Digital Twin. Based on key takeaways from the presented Sydney Opera House case study and previous studies, state DOTs need to consider the following proposed objectives that should be considered for a successful implementation of Digital Twins for a highway system. These objectives include the following:

1. **Improving digital capacity.** State DOTs need to consider having a full data digitization lifecycle from "cradle to cradle" by enhancing digital design and construction, digital operation, and digital data integration with users. Designs should be enabled digitally, integrate automated construction when possible,

and adopt modular design and construction approaches. Moreover, enhancing the digital skills of workers to allow for smart asset management and support customer engagement by improving the digital capabilities of operations.

2. **Understand data architecture**. For each asset, state DOTs need to identify data sources and data requirements, identify the gaps in existing data, and look for additional resources to fill the information gaps.

3. **Set data management plans**. Data specifications and standards, and data governance (i.e., data rules, roles, and responsibilities) should be identified.

4. **Integrate existing management systems**. Structured research and review of any existing information system, such as asset management information systems (AMIS) or any other existing in-house management system whether it is used by the planning division or the maintenance division, should be considered for integration. Additionally, the use of existing databases should be planned for where the newly adopted Digital Twin platform should be designed to support this data integration.

5.3 What is the outcome resulting from the implementation of a holistic Digital Twin for a highway system

Implementing Digital Twins for the highway system will provide an innovative smart management system that integrates asset semantic and geometric data, in addition to spatial data based on the asset location and the surrounding environment. This based Digital Twin management system can support the monitoring and control of the asset condition promptly, employ an advanced machine-learning algorithm to predict the asset condition, and allow for conducting preventive and predictive maintenance.

The developed Digital Twin-based management system will allow for the integration of data extracted from BIM and GIS. BIM can provide rich geometric and semantic asset data including but not limited to asset models (i.e., available 2D models or 3D models), asset specifications, required level of details, asset documentation, data schemes, and ontologies. Additionally, GIS can integrate many types of data while analyzing the spatial location of the asset and organizing layers of information into visualizations using maps and 3D scenes. Moreover, GIS can handle and process spatial data of the individual physical asset, system of assets, and the surrounding environment. The integration of asset data extracted from BIM and GIS can provide a digital representation of the asset architectural entity and will support the management of spatial information of the asset and the surrounding environment, thus providing a better understanding of how the individual physical asset or system of assets interacts with its surrounding [52].

A Digital Twin can reflect the asset condition in a real-time manner; data collected using sensors or cyber-physical-systems (CPS) can also be integrated to allow for comprehensive control and monitoring of the asset or system of assets condition, thus allowing for the early detection of abnormalities and therefore enhancing preventive maintenance. Moreover, the Digital Twin platform can enable the conduction of what-if simulations by utilizing the digitally enhanced asset models, aggregated asset historical data, real-time data, and data related to factors that might affect the asset performance, for instance, data related to the temperature of the surrounding environment, thus allowing for predictive maintenance by simulating the future asset condition based on multi-sourced high quality and reliable data.

The Digital Twin-based management system will result in creating one source of true data, and the generation of a repository environment with simulation capabilities by making use of existing databases and systems. This data management system will release data from isolated silos, improve visualizations, enhance safety, optimize asset performance, allow for better resource allocation, and support data-driven decision-making.

6. Conclusions

Governments and organizations worldwide are investigating innovative approaches to change the design and delivery of civil infrastructure systems, with the ultimate objective of constructing and operating more resilient and sustainable infrastructure that would support equity, enhance safety, and target urbanization. This aim was further emphasized with the shift toward digitizing assets to leverage the value of asset data and optimize the performance of infrastructure assets. As such, the concept of smart infrastructure emerged, that is, connecting the physical aspect of the assets with its digital aspect by the bidirectional communication of information. Smart infrastructure also aligns with the concept of Digital Twins, or the digital representation of physical assets. Given the potential of Digital Twins, several organizations, researchers, and practitioners investigated the implementation of the concept in the civil infrastructure industry.

The concept of Digital Twins in the civil infrastructure industry is not mature yet; however, the adoption of the concept was investigated to address several problems related mainly to the operation and management of infrastructure systems. Few studies have investigated the implementation of Digital Twins throughout the lifecycle of infrastructure projects, but these studies mainly presented a framework for implementation. Additionally, Digital Twins can be applied at different spatial scales including the national level such as the National Digital Twin (NDT) initiative by the UK, on the city level to help with urban planning such as Virtual Singapore and BRISE-Vienna, or for a network of assets such as the vision for Digital Roads or the implementation of Digital Twins as a management information system.

This chapter also presented the journey toward a holistic Digital Twin for a highway system. The Why, How, and What components were investigated. A holistic Digital Twin will support managing cross-asset systems, and how they interact with each other and with the surrounding environment. Moreover, to understand how to translate the vision to practice, a case study related to the implementation of BIM for facility management of the Sydney Opera House was presented and recommendations on implementing a holistic Digital Twin for a highway system were discussed. Finally, data integration between BIM and GIS with the aid of the integration of real-time data about the asset condition, and employment of machine learning algorithm was proposed for a successful implementation of a Digital Twin-based management system that can integrate existing subsystems and make use of existing databases. The proposed smart data management system will allow for conducting preventive and predictive maintenance, support visualization, release data from isolated silos, allow for feasible access to data by creating one source of true data, and enhance decision-making to optimize the overall performance of the highway system.

Acknowledgements

The authors would like to thank Dr. Graham Kelly, director at BIM Academy for providing information about the presented case study.

Author details

Ashtarout Ammar*, Hala Nassereddine and Gabriel Dadi
University of Kentucky, Lexington, KY, USA

*Address all correspondence to: ashtrout.ammar@uky.edu

IntechOpen

© 2022 The Author(s). Licensee IntechOpen. This chapter is distributed under the terms of the Creative Commons Attribution License (http://creativecommons.org/licenses/by/3.0), which permits unrestricted use, distribution, and reproduction in any medium, provided the original work is properly cited.

References

[1] WHO Coronavirus (COVID-19) Dashboard [Internet]. World Health Organization. 2022. Available from: https://covid19. who.int/ [Accessed: 8 August 2022]

[2] Tonne C. Lessons from the COVID-19 pandemic for accelerating sustainable development. Environmental Research. 2021;**193**:110482

[3] Ogunbiyi D. Opinion: Power in a pandemic—Why energy access matters during coronavirus [Internet]. 2020. Available from: https://news.trust.org/item/20200331134807-w6a0h/ [Accessed: 8 August 2022]

[4] Saldinger A. AIIB launches health infrastructure investments in response to COVID-19 [Internet]. 2020. Available from: https://www.devex.com/news/aiib-launches-health-infrastructure-investments-in-response-to-covid-19-96958 [Accessed: 8 August 2022]

[5] Cheshmehzangi A. Revisiting the built environment: 10 potential development changes and paradigm shifts due to COVID-19. Journal of Urban Management. 2021;**10**(2):166-175

[6] Balasubramanian S, Shukla V, Islam N, Manghat S. Construction industry 4.0 and sustainability: An enabling framework. IEEE Transactions on Engineering Management. 2021:1-19. DOI: 10.1109/TEM.2021.3110427

[7] Forcael E, Ferrari I, Opazo-Vega A, Pulido-Arcas JA. Construction 4.0: A literature review. Sustainability. 2020;**12**(22):9755

[8] HM Government. Industrial Strategy Construction Sector Deal [Internet]. London, United Kingdom. 2018. Available from: https://assets.publishing.service.gov.uk/government/uploads/system/uploads/attachment_data/file/731871/construction-sector-deal-print-single.pdf

[9] ASCE. ASCE Statement on President Biden Signing the Infrastructure Investment and Jobs Act into Law [Internet]. American Society of Civil Engineers. Washington, DC, United States. 2021. Available from: https://www.asce.org/publications-and-news/civil-engineering-source/society-news/article/2021/11/15/asce-statement-on-president-biden-signing-the-infrastructure-investment-and-jobs-act-into-law?utm_campaign=GR-2022-5-20-TWiW%20Email%20Short&utm_medium=email&utm_source=Eloqua [Accessed: 20 July 2021]

[10] Updated Fact Sheet: Bipartisan infrastructure investment and jobs act [Internet]. The White House. 2021. Available from: https://www.whitehouse.gov/briefing-room/statements-releases/2021/08/02/updated-fact-sheet-bipartisan-infrastructure-investment-and-jobs-act/#:~:text=The%20bipartisan%20%20Infrastructure%20Investment%20%20and%20Jobs%20Act%20will%20%20invest%20%24110,of%20committee%20%20earlier%20this%20year [Accessed: 20 July 2021]

[11] Obando S. Construction Techies Laud $100M in Infrastructure Act, Push for More [Internet]. Construction Dive. Washington, D.C., United States. 2021. Available from: https://www.constructiondive.com/news/construction-tech-praise-110-million-infrastructure-bill-push-for-more/610126/

[12] Bowers KA, Buscher, Dentten R, Edwards MB, England J, Enzer M, et al. Smart Infrastructure Getting more from strategic assets. [Internet]. Centre for Smart Infrastructure and Construction. 2016. Available from: https://www-smartinfrastructure.eng.cam.ac.uk/system/files/documents/the-smart-infrastructure-paper.pdf

[13] Bolton A, Butler L, Dabson I, Enzer M, Evans M, Fenemore T, et al. Gemini principles [Internet]. Apollo—University of Cambridge Repository. 2018. Available from: https://www.repository.cam.ac.uk/handle/1810/284889 [Accessed: 11 December 2021]

[14] Ammar A, Nassereddine H, AbdulBakyN,AbouKansourA,TannouryJ, Urban H, et al. Digital Twins in the construction industry: A perspective of practitioners and building authority. Frontiers in Built Environment. 2022;**8**:834671

[15] Ammar A, Nassereddine H. Blueprint for construction 4.0 technologies: A bibliometric analysis. IOP Conference Series: Materials Science and Engineering. 2022;**1218**(1):012011

[16] Niederer SA, Sacks MS, Girolami M, Willcox K. Scaling Digital Twins from the artisanal to the industrial. Nature Computational Science. 2021;**1**(5): 313-320

[17] Negri E, Fumagalli L, Macchi M. A review of the roles of Digital Twin in CPS-based production systems. Procedia Manufacturing. 2017;**11**:939-948

[18] Kritzinger W, Karner M, Traar G, Henjes J, Sihn W. Digital Twin in manufacturing: A categorical literature review and classification. IFAC-PapersOnLine. 2018;**51**(11):1016-1022

[19] Tao F, Qi Q, Wang L, Nee AYC. Digital Twins and cyber-physical systems toward smart manufacturing and industry 4.0: Correlation and comparison. Engineering. 2019;**5**(4):653-661

[20] Wanasinghe TR, Wroblewski L, Petersen BK, Gosine RG, James LA, De Silva O, et al. Digital Twin for the oil and gas industry: Overview, research trends, opportunities, and challenges. IEEE Access. 2020;**8**:104175-104197

[21] Brilakis I, Pan Y, Borrmann A, Mayer HG, Rhein F, Vos C, et al. Built environment Digital Twinning. In: Report of the International Workshop on Built Environment Digital Twinning Presented by TUM Institute for Advanced Study and Siemens AG. Germany: Technical University of Munich; 2019

[22] Vieira J, Poças Martins J, Marques de Almeida N, Patrício H, Gomes MJ. Towards resilient and sustainable rail and road networks: A systematic literature review on Digital Twins. Sustainability. 2022;**14**(12):7060

[23] Broo DG, Schooling J. Digital Twins in infrastructure: Definitions, current practices, challenges and strategies. International Journal of Construction Management. 2021:1-10. DOI: 10.1080/15623599.2021.1966980

[24] Callcut M, Cerceau Agliozzo JP, Varga L, McMillan L. Digital Twins in civil infrastructure systems. Sustainability. 2021;**13**(20):11549

[25] Costin A, Adibfar A, Hu H, Chen SS. Building information modeling (BIM) for transportation infrastructure—Literature review, applications, challenges, and recommendations. Automation in Construction. 2018;**94**:257-281

[26] Shim CS, Dang NS, Lon S, Jeon CH. Development of a bridge maintenance

system for prestressed concrete bridges using 3D Digital Twin model. Structure and Infrastructure Engineering. 2019;**15**(10):1319-1332

[27] Jiang F, Ding Y, Song Y, Geng F, Wang Z. An architecture of lifecycle fatigue management of steel bridges driven by Digital Twin. Structural Monitoring and Maintenance. 2021;**8**(2):187-201

[28] Kampczyk A, Dybeł K. The fundamental approach of the Digital Twin application in railway turnouts with innovative monitoring of weather conditions. Sensors. 2021;**21**(17):5757

[29] Kochan A. Digital Twin concept of the ETCS application. WUT Journal of Transportation Engineering. 2020;**131**: 87-98

[30] Kim J, Kim SA. Lifespan prediction technique for Digital Twin-based noise barrier tunnels. Sustainability. 2020;**12**(7):2940

[31] Yu G, Wang Y, Mao Z, Hu M, Sugumaran V, Wang YK. A Digital Twin-based decision analysis framework for operation and maintenance of tunnels. Tunnelling and Underground Space Technology. 2021;**116**:104125

[32] Yu G, Zhang S, Hu M, Wang YK. Prediction of highway tunnel pavement performance based on Digital Twin and multiple time series stacking. Lin JR, editor. Advances in Civil Engineering. 2020;**2020**:1-21

[33] Meža S, Mauko Pranjić A, Vezočnik R, Osmokrović I, Lenart S. Digital Twins and road construction using secondary raw materials. Biancardo SA, editor. Journal of Advanced Transportation. 2021;**2021**:1-12

[34] Rounds D. Design for maintainability: The importance of operations and maintenance considerations during the design phase of construction projects [Internet]. Whole Building Design Guide. 2018. Available from: https://www.wbdg.org/resources/design-for-maintainability [Accessed: 20 August 2022]

[35] National Infrastructure Commission. Data for the Public Good [Internet]. London, United Kingdom. 2017. Available from: https://nic.org.uk/app/uploads/Data-for-the-Public-Good-NIC-Report.pdf

[36] Deloitte. New technologies case study: Data sharing in infrastructure [Internet]. London, United Kingdom. 2017. Available from: https://nic.org.uk/app/uploads//Data-sharing-in-infrastructure.pdf

[37] Ider Batbayar. Virtual Singapore: A Digital "Twin" For Planning [Internet]. 2022. Available from: https://city2city.network/virtual-singapore-digital-twin-planning-innovation-type-institutional-pioneer [Accessed: 10 August 2022]

[38] National Highways. Digital Roads [Internet]. Birmingham, United Kingdom. 2021. Available from: https://nationalhighways.co.uk/media/2chotw13/introducing-digital-roads.pdf

[39] National Highways.Digital Roads 2025 Roadmap [Internet]. Birmingham, United Kingdom. 2021. Available from: https://nationalhighways.co.uk/media/r3nn1h3m/digital-roads-2025-interactive-roadmap_final.pdf

[40] Ammar A, Nassereddine H, Dadi G. State departments of transportation's vision toward Digital Twins: Investigation of roadside asset data management current practices and future requirements. ISPRS Annals of the Photogrammetry, Remote Sensing and Spatial Information Sciences. 2022;**V-4-2022**:319-327

[41] Utah Department of Transporation (UDOT). Digital Twin Strategic Plan [Internet]. Taylorsville, Utah, United States. 2021

[42] AASHTO TAM Guide [Internet]. American Association of State Highway Transportation Officials (AASHTO). Washington, D.C., United States. 2022 Available from: https://www.tamguide.com/guide/

[43] Federal Highway Administration (FHWA). Handbook for Including Ancillary Assets in Transportation Asset Management Programs [Internet]. Washington, DC, United States. 2019. Available from: https://www.fhwa.dot.gov/publications/research/infrastructure/19068/19068.pdf

[44] Le T, Le C, David Jeong H. Lifecycle data modeling to support transferring project-oriented data to asset-oriented systems in transportation projects. Journal of Management in Engineering. 2018;**34**(4):04018024

[45] National Academies of Sciences, Engineering, and Medicine. Guidebook for Data and Information Systems for Transportation Asset Management. Washington, DC, United States: The National Academies Press; 2021. DOI: 10.17226/26126

[46] Ammar A, Dadi G, Nassereddine H. Transportation asset data management: BIM as a holistic data management approach. In: Construction Research Congress 2022 [Internet]. Arlington, Virginia: American Society of Civil Engineers; 2022. pp. 208-217. Available from: http://ascelibrary.org/doi/10.1061/9780784483954.022 [Accessed: 8 August 2022]

[47] Rahn PK. State DOT Mission Evolution. American Association of State Highway and Transportation Officials (AASHTO). Washington, DC, United States. 2013. p. 30 Report No.: NCHRP Project 20-24 (84)

[48] Marczyk GR, DeMatteo D, Festinger D. Essentials of research design and methodology. Hoboken, New Jersey, United States: John Wiley & Sons; 2010

[49] Sydney Opera House [Internet]. 2022. Available from: https://www.gatherlearning.com/institutions/sydney-opera-house [Accessed: 12 August 2022]

[50] Interesting Facts About the Sydney Opera House [Internet]. 2022. Available from: https://www.sydneyoperahouse.com/our-story/sydney-opera-house-facts.html [Accessed: 12 August 2022]

[51] Elaine Knutt. Sydney Opera House Trials New BIM for F.M. Service [Internet]. 2014. Available from: https://www.bimplus.co.uk/sydney-ope5ra-hous2e-tria1ls-new-bim-fm-service/ [Accessed: 12 August 2022]

[52] Ammar A, Dadi G. Towards an integrated Building Information Modeling (BIM) and Geographic Information System (GIS) platform for infrastructure. In: Feng C, Linner T, Brilakis I, Castro D, Chen PH, Cho Y, et al., editors. Proceedings of the 38th International Symposium on Automation and Robotics in Construction (ISARC). Dubai, UAE: International Association for Automation and Robotics in Construction (IAARC); 2021. pp. 129-136